THE
TWILIGHT OF
THE IDOLS
AND THE ANTICHRIST

THE TWILIGHT OF THE IDOLS

THE IDOLS

AND THE ANTICHRIST

FRIEDRICH NIETZSCHE

Translated by Anthony M. Ludovici

This edition published in 2024 by Arcturus Publishing Limited
26/27 Bickels Yard, 151–153 Bermondsey Street,
London SE1 3HA

Cover design: Peter Ridley

AD011749UK

Printed in the UK

CONTENTS

INTRODUCTION

Born in eastern Germany in 1844, Friedrich Wilhelm Nietzsche is considered to have been one of Europe's greatest and most controversial thinkers. Nietzsche's father, Carl Ludwig Nietzsche was a Lutheran pastor and former teacher who died from a sudden illness in 1849 when Nietzsche was just four years old.

As a boy, Nietzsche attended a private school where he did particularly well in Christian theology. Later, in 1858, he was offered a scholarship to study at Schulpforta, a school located in a former Cistercian monastery.

Nietzsche's time at Shulpforta not only provided him a grounding in languages such as Greek, Latin, Hebrew and French, but allowed him the independence that came with living away from family. Having excelled in his studies, Nietzsche graduated from Schulpforta in 1864 and went on to study theology and classical philology at the University of Bonn. Despite his recent successes in education, he struggled to adjust at Bonn and transferred a year later to the University of Leipzig. Around the same time, F. W. Ritschl, a leading classical scholar and one of Nietzsche's professors had also accepted an appointment at Leipzig. At Leipzig, Nietzsche thrived as a student, enjoying Ritschl's renowned instruction and becoming the only student to publish in his journal *Rheinisches Museum*.

After a pause in his studies and a stint in military service that ended with a serious chest injury, Nietzsche returned to Leipzig in October 1868 and continued his studies. A year later, when a professorship in classical philology became available at the University of Basel, Ritschl's recommendation and support of Nietzsche resulted in him becoming the youngest Chair of Classical Philology at the institution. Aged just 24, he was also offered an honorary doctorate by Leipzig University.

In the years following, Nietzsche's focus on classical philology and theology led to the writing and publication of *The Birth of Tragedy*, a book of essays on the artistic, religious and philosophical interpretations of classical Athenian tragedy. This book, like many of his works, was widely criticised by readers and scholars of the subject who believed Nietzsche had shown his ignorance and 'complete misunderstanding' of the subject in question. Never shy of criticism, Nietzsche was known for responding to such allegations and defending his work. His most famous work, *Thus Spake Zarathustra*, was published in 1883 and put forth highly controversial ideas regarding the 'death of God' and man's will to break free of religious thought.

Known today for his philosophical writings and criticisms of culture, much of Nietzsche's analyses covered topics such as religion, art and science, among others, and dealt with ideas of morality, individualism and self-overcoming. This volume, translated by Anthony M. Ludovici, is titled *The Twilight of the Idols and The Antichrist*, and contains a range of his later works. While *The Twilight of the Idols* includes criticisms of German culture, as well as other European practices, *The Antichrist* introduces philosophical concepts such as 'will to power'. Also included in this volume is Nietzsche's essay 'The Eternal Recurrence' and his 'Explanatory Notes to *Thus Spake Zarathustra*'.

Throughout his life, Nietzsche experienced bouts of severe depression and in later years, suffered multiple strokes and psychosis. In the summer of 1900, he contracted pneumonia and died on 25 August after another stroke.

Born in 1882, Anthony M. Ludovici was a British philosopher, social critic and author fluent in several languages including German. Upon publication in 1911, this edition was referred to as 'the first complete and authorised English translation' of these texts.

THE TWILIGHT OF
THE IDOLS

TRANSLATOR'S PREFACE

The Twilight of the Idols was written towards the end of the summer of 1888. Its composition seems to have occupied only a few days – so few indeed that, in *Ecce Homo* (p. 118), Nietzsche says he hesitates to give their number; but, in any case, we know it was completed on the 3rd of September in Sils Maria. The manuscript which was dispatched to the printers on the 7th of September bore the title: '*Idle Hours of a Psychologist*'; this, however, was abandoned in favour of the present title, while the work was going through the press. During September and the early part of October 1888, Nietzsche added to the original contents of the book by inserting the whole section entitled 'Things the Germans Lack', and aphorisms 32–43 of 'Skirmishes in a War with the Age'; and the book, as it now stands, represents exactly the form in which Nietzsche intended to publish it in the course of the year 1889. Unfortunately its author was already stricken down with illness when the work first appeared at the end of January 1889, and he was denied the joy of seeing it run into nine editions, of one thousand each, before his death in 1900.

Of *The Twilight of the Idols*, Nietzsche says in *Ecce Homo* (p. 118): – 'If anyone should desire to obtain a rapid sketch of how everything before my time was standing on its head, he should begin reading me in this book. That which is called "Idols" on the title-page is simply the old truth that has been believed in hitherto. In plain English, *The Twilight of the Idols* means that the old truth is on its last legs.'

Certain it is that, for a rapid survey of the whole of Nietzsche's doctrine, no book, save perhaps the section entitled 'Of Old and New Tables' in *Thus Spake Zarathustra*, could be of more real value than *The Twilight of the Idols*. Here Nietzsche is quite at his best. He is ripe for the marvellous feat of the transvaluation of all values. Nowhere is his language – that marvellous weapon which in his hand became

11

at once so supple and so murderous – more forcible and more condensed. Nowhere are his thoughts more profound. But all this does not by any means imply that this book is the easiest of Nietzsche's works. On the contrary, I very much fear that, unless the reader is well prepared, not only in Nietzscheism, but also in the habit of grappling with uncommon and elusive problems, a good deal of the contents of this work will tend rather to confuse than to enlighten him in regard to what Nietzsche actually wishes to make clear in these pages.

How much prejudice, for instance, how many traditional and deep-seated opinions, must be uprooted, if we are to see even so much as an important note of interrogation in the section entitled 'The Problem of Socrates' – not to speak of such sections as 'Morality as the Enemy of Nature', 'The Four Great Errors', &c. The errors exposed in these sections have a tradition of two thousand years behind them; and only a fantastic dreamer could expect them to be eradicated by a mere casual study of these pages. Indeed, Nietzsche himself looked forward only to a gradual change in the general view of the questions he discussed; he knew only too well what the conversion of 'light heads' was worth, and what kind of man would probably be the first to rush into his arms; and, grand psychologist that he was, he guarded himself beforehand against bad company by means of his famous warning: 'The first adherents of a creed do not prove anything against it.'

To the aspiring student of Nietzsche, however, it ought not to be necessary to become an immediate convert in order to be interested in the treasure of thought which Nietzsche here lavishes upon us. For such a man it will be quite difficult enough to regard the questions raised in this work as actual problems. Once, however, he has succeeded in doing this, and has given his imagination time to play round these questions as problems, the particular turn or twist that Nietzsche gives to their elucidation, may then perhaps strike him, not only as valuable, but as absolutely necessary.

With regard to the substance of *The Twilight of the Idols*, Nietzsche says in *Ecce Homo* (p. 119): 'There is the waste of an all-too-rich autumn in this book: you trip over truths. You even crush some to death, there are too many of them.'

And what are these truths? They are things that are not yet held to be true. They are the utterances of a man who, as a single exception, escaped for a while the general insanity of Europe, with its blind idealism in the midst of squalor, with its unscrupulous praise of so-called 'Progress' while it stood knee-deep in the belittlement of 'Man', and with its vulgar levity in the face of effeminacy and decay; – they are the utterances of one who voiced the hopes, the aims, and the realities of another world, not of an ideal world, not of a world beyond, but of a real world, of this world regenerated and reorganised upon a sounder, a more virile, and a more orderly basis, – in fact, of a perfectly *possible* world, one that has already existed in the past, and could exist again, if only the stupendous revolution of a transvaluation of all values were made possible.

This then is the nature of the truths uttered by this one sane man in the whole of Europe at the end of last century; and when, owing to his unequal struggle against the overwhelming hostile forces of his time, his highly sensitive personality was at last forced to surrender itself to the enemy and become one with them – that is to say, insane! – at least the record of his sanity had been safely stored away, beyond the reach of time and change, in the volumes which constitute his life-work.

*****

Nietzsche must have started upon the 'Antichrist', immediately after having dispatched the 'Idle Hours of a Psychologist' to the printers, and the work appears to have been finished at the end of September 1888. It was intended by Nietzsche to form the first book of a large work entitled 'The Transvaluation of all Values'; but, though this work was never completed, we can form some idea from the substance of the 'Antichrist' and from the titles of the remaining three books, which alas! were never written, of what its contents would have been. These titles are: Book II. The Free Spirit. A Criticism of Philosophy as a Nihilistic Movement. Book III. The Immoralist. A Criticism of the most Fatal Kind of Ignorance – Morality. Book IV. Dionysus. The Philosophy of Eternal Recurrence.

Nietzsche calls this book 'An Attempted Criticism of Christianity'. Modest as this sub-title is, it will probably seem not quite modest enough to those who think that Nietzsche fell far short of doing justice to their Holy Creed. Be this as it may, there is the solution of a certain profound problem in this book, which, while it is the key to all Nietzscheism, is also the justification and the sanctification of

Nietzsche's cause. The problem stated quite plainly is this: '*To what end* did Christianity avail itself of falsehood?'

Many readers of this amazing little work, who happen to be acquainted with Nietzsche's doctrine of Art and of Ruling, will probably feel slightly confused at the constant deprecation of falsehood, of deception, and of arbitrary make-believe, which seems to run through this book like a litany in praise of a certain Absolute Truth.

Remembering Nietzsche's utterance in volume ii. (p. 26) of the *Will to Power*, to wit: 'The prerequisite of all living things and of their lives is: that there should be a large amount of faith, that it should be possible to pass definite judgments on things, and that there should be no doubt at all concerning values. Thus it is necessary that something should be assumed to be true, *not* that it is true;' – remembering these words, as I say, the reader may stand somewhat aghast before all those passages in the second half of this volume, where the very falsehoods of Christianity, its assumptions, its unwarrantable claims to Truth, are declared to be pernicious, base and corrupt.

Again and again, if we commit the error of supposing that Nietzsche believed in a truth that was absolute, we shall find throughout his works reasons for charging him with apparently the very same crimes that he here lays at the door of Christianity. What then is the explanation of his seeming inconsistency?

It is simple enough. Nietzsche's charge of falsehood against Christianity is not a moral one, – in fact it may be taken as a general rule that Nietzsche scrupulously avoids making moral charges, and that he remains throughout faithful to his position Beyond Good and Evil (see, for instance Aph. 6 (Antichrist) where he repudiates all moral prejudice in charging humanity with corruption). A man who maintained that 'truth is that form of error which enables a particular species to prevail,' could not make a *moral* charge of falsehood against any one, or any institution; but he could do so from another standpoint He could well say, for instance, 'falsehood is that kind of error which causes a particular species to degenerate and to decay.'

Thus the fact that Christianity 'lied' becomes a subject of alarm to Nietzsche, not owing to the fact that it is immoral to lie, but because in this particular instance, the lie was harmful, hostile to life, and dangerous to humanity; for 'a belief might be false and yet life-preserving' (*Beyond Good and Evil*, pp. 8, 9).

Suppose, therefore, we say with Nietzsche that there is no absolute truth, but that all that has been true in the past which has been the means of making the 'plant man flourish best' – or, since the meaning of 'best' is open to some debate, let us say, flourish in a Nietzschean sense, that is to say, thanks to a mastery of life, and to a preponderance of all those qualities which say yea to existence, and which suggest no flight from this world and all its pleasure and pain. And suppose we add that, wherever we may find the plant man flourishing, in this sense, we should there suspect the existence of truth?! If we say this with Nietzsche, any sort of assumption or arbitrary valuation which aims at a reverse order of things, becomes a dangerous lie in a supermoral and purely physiological sense.

With these preparatory remarks we are now prepared to read aphorism 56 with a complete understanding of what Nietzsche means, and to recognise in this particular aphorism the key to the whole of Nietzsche's attitude towards Christianity. It is at once a solution of our problem, and a justification of its author's position. Naturally, it still remains open to Nietzsche's opponents to argue, if they choose, that man has flourished best under the sway of nihilistic religions – religions which deny life, – and that consequently the falsehoods of Christianity are not only warrantable but also in the highest degree blessed; but, in any case, the aphorism in question completely exonerates Nietzsche from a charge of inconsistency in the use of the terms 'truth' and 'falsehood' throughout his works, and it moreover settles once and for all the exact altitude from which our author looked down upon the religions of the world, not only to criticise them, but also to *place* them in the order of their merit as disciplinary systems aiming at the cultivation of particular types of men.

Nietzsche says in aphorism 56: – 'After all, the question is, to what end are falsehoods perpetrated? The fact that, in Christianity, "holy" ends are entirely absent, constitutes *my* objection to the means it employs. Its ends are only *bad* ends: the poisoning, the calumniation and the denial of life, the contempt of the body, the degradation and self-pollution of man by virtue of the concept sin, – consequently its means are bad as well.'

Thus, to repeat it once more, it is not because Christianity availed itself of all kinds of lies that Nietzsche condemns it; for the Book of Manu – which he admires – is just as full of falsehood as the Semitic

Book of Laws; but, in the Book of Manu the lies are calculated to preserve and to create a strong and noble type of man, whereas in Christianity the opposite type was the aim, – an aim which has been achieved in a manner far exceeding even the expectations of the faithful.

This then is the main argument of the book and its conclusion; but, in the course of the general elaboration of this argument, many important side-issues are touched upon and developed, wherein Nietzsche reveals himself as something very much more valuable than a mere iconoclast. Of course, on every page of his philosophy – whatever his enemies may maintain to the contrary – he never once ceases to construct, since he is incessantly enumerating and emphasising those qualities and types which he fain would rear, as against those he fain would see destroyed; but it is in aphorism 57 of this book that Nietzsche makes the plainest and most complete statement of his actual taste in Sociology, and it is upon this aphorism that all his followers and disciples will ultimately have to build, if Nietzscheism is ever to become something more than a merely intellectual movement.

ANTHONY M. LUDOVICI.

PREFACE

To maintain a cheerful attitude of mind in the midst of a gloomy and exceedingly responsible task, is no slight artistic feat. And yet, what could be more necessary than cheerfulness? Nothing ever succeeds which exuberant spirits have not helped to produce. Surplus power, alone, is the proof of power. A *transvaluation of all values* – this note of interrogation which is so black, so huge, that it casts a shadow even upon him who affixes it – is a task of such fatal import, that he who undertakes it is compelled every now and then to rush out into the sunlight in order to shake himself free from an earnestness that becomes crushing, far too crushing. This end justifies every means, every event on the road to it is a windfall. Above all war. War has always been the great policy of all spirits who have penetrated too far into themselves or who have grown too deep; a wound stimulates the recuperative powers. For many years, a maxim, the origin of which I withhold from learned curiosity, has been my motto:

increscunt animi, virescit volnere virtus.

At other times another means of recovery which is even more to my taste, is to cross-examine idols. There are more idols than realities in the world: this constitutes my 'evil eye' for this world: it is also my 'evil ear'. To put questions in this quarter with a hammer, and to hear perchance that well-known hollow sound which tells of blown-out frogs – what a joy this is for one who has ears even behind his ears, for an old psychologist and Pied Piper like myself in whose presence precisely that which would fain be silent, *must betray itself.*

Even this treatise – as its title shows – is above all a recreation, a ray of sunshine, a leap sideways of a psychologist in his leisure moments. Maybe, too, a new war? And are we again cross-examining new idols? This little work is a great declaration of war; and with regard to the cross-examining of idols, this time it is not the idols of the age but eternal idols which are here struck with a hammer as with a tuning fork – there are certainly no idols which are older, more convinced, and more inflated. Neither are there any more hollow. This does not alter the fact that they are believed in more than any others, besides they are never called idols – at least, not the most exalted among their number.

FRIEDRICH NIETZSCHE.

TURIN, the *30th September* 1888.
on the day when the first
book of the Transvaluation
of all Values was finished.

MAXIMS AND MISSILES

1

Idleness is the parent of all psychology. What? Is psychology then a – vice?

2

Even the pluckiest among us has but seldom the courage of what he really knows.

3

Aristotle says that in order to live alone, a man must be either an animal or a god. The third alternative is lacking: a man must be both – a *philosopher*.

4

'All truth is simple.' – Is not this a double lie?

5

Once for all I wish to be blind to many things. – Wisdom sets bounds even to knowledge.

6

A man recovers best from his exceptional nature – his intellectuality – by giving his animal instincts a chance.

7

Which is it? Is man only a blunder of God? Or is God only a blunder of man?

8

From the military school of life. – That which does not kill me, makes me stronger.

9

Help thyself, then everyone will help thee. A principle of neighbour-love.

10

A man should not play the coward to his deeds. He should not repudiate them once he has performed them. Pangs of conscience are indecent.

11

Can a donkey be tragic? – To perish beneath a load that one can neither bear nor throw off? This is the case of the Philosopher.

12

If a man knows the wherefore of his existence, then the manner of it can take care of itself. Man does not aspire to happiness; only the Englishman does that.

13

Man created woman – out of what? Out of a rib of his god, of his 'ideal'.

14

What? Art thou looking for something? Thou wouldst fain multiply thyself tenfold, a hundredfold? Thou seekest followers? Seek ciphers!

15

Posthumous men, like myself, are not so well understood as men who reflect their age, but they are heard with more respect. In plain English: we are never understood – hence our authority.

16

Among women. – 'Truth? Oh, you do not know truth! Is it not an outrage on all our *pudeurs*?' –

17

There is an artist after my own heart, modest in his needs: he really wants only two things, his bread and his art – *panem et Circem*.

18

He who knows not how to plant his will in things, at least endows them with some meaning: that is to say, he believes that a will is already present in them. (A principle of faith.)

19

What? Ye chose virtue and the heaving breast, and at the same time ye squint covetously at the advantages of the unscrupulous. – But with virtue ye renounce all 'advantages'... (to be nailed to an Antisemite's door).

20

The perfect woman perpetrates literature as if it were a petty vice: as an experiment, *en passant*, and looking about her all the while to see whether anybody is noticing her, hoping that somebody *is* noticing her.

21

One should adopt only those situations in which one is in no need of sham virtues, but rather, like the tight-rope dancer on his tight rope, in which one must either fall or stand – or escape.

22

'Evil men have no songs.'* – How is it that the Russians have songs?

23

'German intellect'; for eighteen years this has been a *contradictio in adjecto*.

---

* This is a reference to Seume's poem 'Die Gesänge', the first verse of which is: –
'Wo man singet, lass dich ruhig nieder,
Ohne Furcht, was man im Lande glaubt;
Wo man singet, wird kein Mensch beraubt:
Bösewichter haben keine Lieder.'
('Wherever people sing thou canst safely settle down without a qualm as to what the general faith of the land may be. Wherever people sing, no man is ever robbed; *rascals* have no songs.') Popular tradition, however, renders the lines thus: –
'Wo man singt, da lass dich ruhig nieder;
Base Menschen [evil men] haben keine Lieder.'

24

By seeking the beginnings of things, a man becomes a crab. The historian looks backwards: in the end he also *believes* backwards.

25

Contentment preserves one even from catching cold. Has a woman who knew that she was well-dressed ever caught cold? – No, not even when she had scarcely a rag to her back.

26

I distrust all systematisers, and avoid them. The will to a system, shows a lack of honesty.

27

Man thinks woman profound – why? Because he can never fathom her depths. Woman is not even shallow.

28

When woman possesses masculine virtues, she is enough to make you run away. When she possesses no masculine virtues, she herself runs away.

29

'How often conscience had to bite in times gone by! What good teeth it must have had! And today, what is amiss?' – A dentist's question.

30

Errors of haste are seldom committed singly. The first time a man always does too much. And precisely on that account he commits a second error, and then he does too little.

31

The trodden worm curls up. This testifies to its caution. It thus reduces its chances of being trodden upon again. In the language of morality: Humility. –

32

There is such a thing as a hatred of lies and dissimulation, which is the outcome of a delicate sense of humour; there is also the selfsame hatred but as the result of cowardice, in so far as falsehood is forbidden by Divine law. Too cowardly to lie....

33

What trifles constitute happiness! The sound of a bagpipe. Without music life would be a mistake. The German imagines even God as a songster.

34

On ne peut penser et écrire qu'assis (G. Flaubert). Here I have got you, you nihilist! A sedentary life is the real sin against the Holy Spirit. Only those thoughts that come by walking have any value.

35

There are times when we psychologists are like horses, and grow fretful. We see our own shadow rise and fall before us. The psychologist must look away from himself if he wishes to see anything at all.

36

Do we immoralists injure virtue in any way? Just as little as the anarchists injure royalty. Only since they have been shot at do princes sit firmly on their thrones once more. Moral: *morality must be shot at.*

37

Thou runnest *ahead*? – Dost thou do so as a shepherd or as an exception? A third alternative would be the fugitive.... First question of conscience.

38

Art thou genuine or art thou only an actor? Art thou a representative or the thing represented, itself? Finally, art thou perhaps simply a copy of an actor?... Second question of conscience.

39

The disappointed man speaks: – I sought for great men, but all I found were the apes of their ideal.

40

Art thou one who looks on, or one who puts his own shoulder to the wheel? – Or art thou one who looks away, or who turns aside?... Third question of conscience.

41

Wilt thou go in company, or lead, or go by thyself?... A man should know what he desires, and that he desires something. – Fourth question of conscience.

42

They were but rungs in my ladder, on them I made my ascent: – to that end I had to go beyond them. But they imagined that I wanted to lay myself to rest upon them.

43

What matters it whether I am acknowledged to be right! I am much too right. And he who laughs best today, will also laugh last.

44

The formula of my happiness: a Yea, a Nay, a straight line, *goal*....

THE PROBLEM OF SOCRATES

1

In all ages the wisest have always agreed in their judgment of life: *it is no good*. At all times and places the same words have been on their lips, – words full of doubt, full of melancholy, full of weariness of life, full of hostility to life. Even Socrates' dying words were: 'To live – means to be ill a long while: I owe a cock to the god Æsculapius.' Even Socrates had had enough of it. What does that prove? What does it point to? Formerly people would have said (– oh, it has been said, and loudly enough too; by our Pessimists loudest of all!): 'In any case there must be some truth in this! The *consensus sapientium* is a proof of truth.' – Shall we say the same today? *May* we do so? 'In any case there must be some sickness here,' we make reply. These great sages of all periods should first be examined more closely! Is it possible that they were, every one of them, a little shaky on their legs, effete, rocky, decadent? Does wisdom perhaps appear on earth after the manner of a crow attracted by a slight smell of carrion?

2

This irreverent belief that the great sages were decadent types, first occurred to me precisely in regard to that case concerning which both learned and vulgar prejudice was most opposed to my view. I recognised Socrates and Plato as symptoms of decline, as instruments in the disintegration of Hellas, as pseudo-Greek, as anti-Greek (*The Birth of Tragedy*, 1872). That *consensus sapientium*, as I perceived ever more and more clearly, did not in the least prove that they were right in the matter on which they agreed. It proved rather that these sages themselves must have been alike in some physiological particular, in order to assume the same negative attitude towards life – in order to be bound to assume that attitude. After all, judgments and valuations of life, whether for or against, cannot be true: their only value lies in the fact that they are symptoms; they can be considered only as symptoms,

– *per se* such judgments are nonsense. You must therefore endeavour by all means to reach out and try to grasp this astonishingly subtle axiom, *that the value of life cannot be estimated*. A living man cannot do so, because he is a contending party, or rather the very object in the dispute, and not a judge; nor can a dead man estimate it – for other reasons. For a philosopher to see a problem in the value of life, is almost an objection against him, a note of interrogation set against his wisdom – a lack of wisdom. What? Is it possible that all these great sages were not only decadents, but that they were not even wise? Let me however return to the problem of Socrates.

3

To judge from his origin, Socrates belonged to the lowest of the low: Socrates was mob. You know, and you can still see it for yourself, how ugly he was. But ugliness, which in itself is an objection, was almost a refutation among the Greeks. Was Socrates really a Greek? Ugliness is not infrequently the expression of thwarted development, or of development arrested by crossing. In other cases it appears as a decadent development. The anthropologists among the criminal specialists declare that the typical criminal is ugly: *monstrum in fronte, monstrum in animo*. But the criminal is a decadent.[*] Was Socrates a typical criminal? – At all events this would not clash with that famous physiognomist's judgment which was so repugnant to Socrates' friends. While on his way through Athens a certain foreigner who was no fool at judging by looks, told Socrates to his face that he was a monster, that his body harboured all the worst vices and passions. And Socrates replied simply: 'You know me, sir!'

4

Not only are the acknowledged wildness and anarchy of Socrates' instincts indicative of decadence, but also that preponderance of the logical faculties and that malignity of the misshapen which was his special characteristic. Neither should we forget those aural delusions which were religiously interpreted as 'the demon of Socrates'. Everything in him is exaggerated, *buffo*, caricature, his nature is also full of concealment, of

---

[*] It should be borne in mind that Nietzsche recognised two types of criminals, – the criminal from strength, and the criminal from weakness. This passage alludes to the latter, Aphorism 45, p. 87, alludes to the former. – TR.

ulterior motives, and of underground currents. I try to understand the idiosyncrasy from which the Socratic equation: – Reason = Virtue = Happiness, could have arisen: the weirdest equation ever seen, and one which was essentially opposed to all the instincts of the older Hellenes.

5

With Socrates Greek taste veers round in favour of dialectics: what actually occurs? In the first place a noble taste is vanquished: with dialectics the mob comes to the top. Before Socrates' time, dialectical manners were avoided in good society: they were regarded as bad manners, they were compromising. Young men were cautioned against them. All such proffering of one's reasons was looked upon with suspicion. Honest things like honest men do not carry their reasons on their sleeve in such fashion. It is not good form to make a show of everything. That which needs to be proved cannot be worth much. Wherever authority still belongs to good usage, wherever men do not prove but command, the dialectician is regarded as a sort of clown. People laugh at him, they do not take him seriously. Socrates was a clown who succeeded in making men take him seriously: what then was the matter?

6

A man resorts to dialectics only when he has no other means to hand. People know that they excite suspicion with it and that it is not very convincing. Nothing is more easily dispelled than a dialectical effect: this is proved by the experience of every gathering in which discussions are held. It can be only the last defence of those who have no other weapons. One must require to extort one's right, otherwise one makes no use of it. That is why the Jews were dialecticians. Reynard the Fox was a dialectician: what? – and was Socrates one as well?

7

Is the Socratic irony an expression of revolt, of mob resentment? Does Socrates, as a creature suffering under oppression, enjoy his innate ferocity in the knife-thrusts of the syllogism? Does he wreak his revenge on the noblemen he fascinates? – As a dialectician a man has a merciless instrument to wield; he can play the tyrant with it: he compromises when he conquers with it. The dialectician leaves it to his opponent to prove that he is no idiot: he infuriates, he likewise paralyses. The dialectician cripples the intellect of his opponent. Can it be that dialectics was only a form of revenge in Socrates?

8

I have given you to understand in what way Socrates was able to repel: now it is all the more necessary to explain how he fascinated. – One reason is that he discovered a new kind of *Agon*, and that he was the first fencing-master in the best circles in Athens. He fascinated by appealing to the combative instinct of the Greeks, – he introduced a variation into the contests between men and youths. Socrates was also a great erotic.

9

But Socrates divined still more. He saw right through his noble Athenians; he perceived that his case, his peculiar case, was no exception even in his time. The same kind of degeneracy was silently preparing itself everywhere: ancient Athens was dying out. And Socrates understood that the whole world needed him – his means, his remedy, his special artifice for self-preservation. Everywhere the instincts were in a state of anarchy; everywhere people were within an ace of excess: the *monstrum in animo* was the general danger. 'The instincts would play the tyrant; we must discover a counter-tyrant who is stronger than they.' On the occasion when that physiognomist had unmasked Socrates, and had told him what he was, a crater full of evil desires, the great Master of Irony let fall one or two words more, which provide the key to his nature. 'This is true,' he said, 'but I overcame them all.' How did Socrates succeed in mastering himself? His case was at bottom only the extreme and most apparent example of a state of distress which was beginning to be general: that state in which no one was able to master himself and in which the instincts turned one against the other. As the extreme example of this state, he fascinated – his terrifying ugliness made him conspicuous to every eye: it is quite obvious that he fascinated still more as a reply, as a solution, as an apparent cure of this case.

10

When a man finds it necessary, as Socrates did, to create a tyrant out of reason, there is no small danger that something else wishes to play the tyrant. Reason was then discovered as a saviour; neither Socrates nor his 'patients' were at liberty to be rational or not, as they pleased; at that time it was *de rigueur*, it had become a last shift. The fanaticism with which the whole of Greek thought plunges into reason, betrays a critical condition of things: men were in danger; there were only two alternatives: either perish or else be absurdly rational. The moral bias of Greek philosophy from Plato onward, is the outcome of a pathological condition, as is also its appreciation of dialectics. Reason = Virtue = Happiness, simply means: we must imitate Socrates, and confront the dark passions permanently with the light of day – the light of reason. We must at all costs be clever, precise, clear: all yielding to the instincts, to the unconscious, leads downwards.

11

I have now explained how Socrates fascinated: he seemed to be a doctor, a Saviour. Is it necessary to expose the errors which lay in his faith in 'reason at any price'? – It is a piece of self-deception on the part of philosophers and moralists to suppose that they can extricate themselves from degeneration by merely waging war upon it. They cannot thus extricate themselves; that which they choose as a means, as the road to salvation, is in itself again only an expression of degeneration – they only modify its mode of manifesting itself: they do not abolish it. Socrates was a misunderstanding. *The whole of the morality of amelioration – that of Christianity as well – was a misunderstanding.* The most blinding light of day: reason at any price; life made clear, cold, cautious, conscious, without instincts, opposed to the instincts, was in itself only a disease, another kind of disease – and by no means a return to 'virtue', to 'health', and to happiness. To be obliged to fight the instincts – this is the formula of degeneration: as long as life is in the ascending line, happiness is the same as instinct.

12

Did he understand this himself, this most intelligent of self-deceivers? Did he confess this to himself in the end, in the wisdom of his courage before death. Socrates wished to die. Not Athens, but his own hand gave him the draught of hemlock; he drove Athens to the poisoned cup. 'Socrates is not a doctor,' he whispered to himself, 'death alone can be a doctor here.... Socrates himself has only been ill a long while.'

'REASON' IN PHILOSOPHY

1

You ask me what all idiosyncrasy is in philosophers?... For instance their lack of the historical sense, their hatred even of the idea of Becoming, their Egyptianism. They imagine that they do honour to a thing by divorcing it from history *sub specie æterni*, – when they make a mummy of it. All the ideas that philosophers have treated for thousands of years, have been mummied concepts; nothing real has ever come out of their hands alive. These idolaters of concepts merely kill and stuff things when they worship, – they threaten the life of everything they adore. Death, change, age, as well as procreation and growth, are in their opinion objections, – even refutations. That which is cannot evolve; that which evolves *is* not. Now all of them believe, and even with desperation, in Being. But, as they cannot lay hold of it, they try to discover reasons why this privilege is withheld from them. 'Some merely apparent quality, some deception must be the cause of our not being able to ascertain the nature of Being: where is the deceiver?' 'We have him,' they cry rejoicing, 'it is sensuality!' These senses, *which in other things are so immoral*, cheat us concerning the true world. Moral: we must get rid of the deception of the senses, of Becoming, of history, of falsehood. – History is nothing more than the belief in the senses, the belief in falsehood. Moral: we must say 'no' to everything in which the senses believe: to all the rest of mankind: all that belongs to the 'people'. Let us be philosophers, mummies, monotono-theists, grave-diggers! – And above all, away with the *body*, this wretched *idée fixe* of the senses, infected with all the faults of logic that exist, refuted, even impossible, although it be impudent enough to pose as if it were real!

2

With a feeling of great reverence I except the name of *Heraclitus*. If the rest of the philosophic gang rejected the evidences of the senses, because the latter revealed a state of multifariousness and change, he rejected the same evidence because it revealed things as if they possessed permanence and unity. Even Heraclitus did an injustice to the senses. The latter lie neither as the Eleatics believed them to lie, nor as he believed them to lie, – they do not lie at all. The interpretations we give to their evidence is what first introduces falsehood into it; for instance the lie of unity, the lie of matter, of substance and of permanence. Reason is the cause of our falsifying the evidence of the senses. In so far as the senses show us a state of Becoming, of transiency, and of change, they do not lie. But in declaring that Being was an empty illusion, Heraclitus will remain eternally right. The 'apparent' world is the only world: the 'true world' is no more than a false adjunct thereto.

3

And what delicate instruments of observation we have in our senses! This human nose, for instance, of which no philosopher has yet spoken with reverence and gratitude, is, for the present, the most finely adjusted instrument at our disposal: it is able to register even such slight changes of movement as the spectroscope would be unable to record. Our scientific triumphs at the present day extend precisely so far as we have accepted the evidence of our senses, – as we have sharpened and armed them, and learned to follow them up to the end. What remains is abortive and not yet science – that is to say, metaphysics, theology, psychology, epistemology, or formal science, or a doctrine of symbols, like logic and its applied form mathematics. In all these things reality does not come into consideration at all, even as a problem; just as little as does the question concerning the general value of such a convention of symbols as logic.

4

The other idiosyncrasy of philosophers is no less dangerous; it consists in confusing the last and the first things. They place that which makes its appearance last – unfortunately! for it ought not to appear at all! – the 'highest concept', that is to say, the most general, the emptiest, the last cloudy streak of evaporating reality, at the beginning as the beginning. This again is only their manner of expressing their veneration: the highest thing must not have grown out of the lowest, it must not have grown at all.... Moral: everything of the first rank must be *causa sui*. To have been derived from something else, is as good as an objection, it sets the value of a thing in question. All superior values are of the first rank, all the highest concepts – that of Being, of the Absolute, of Goodness, of Truth, and of Perfection; all these things cannot have been evolved, they must therefore be *causa sui*. All these things cannot however be unlike one another, they cannot be opposed to one another. Thus they attain to their stupendous concept 'God'. The last, most attenuated and emptiest thing is postulated as the first thing, as the absolute cause, as *ens realissimum*. Fancy humanity having to take the brain diseases of morbid cobweb-spinners seriously! – And it has paid dearly for having done so.

<h1 style="text-align:center">5</h1>

Against this let us set the different manner in which we (you observe that I am courteous enough to say 'we') conceive the problem of the error and deceptiveness of things. Formerly people regarded change and evolution in general as the proof of appearance, as a sign of the fact that something must be there that leads us astray. Today, on the other hand, we realise that precisely as far as the rational bias forces us to postulate unity, identity, permanence, substance, cause, materiality and being, we are in a measure involved in error, driven necessarily to error; however certain we may feel, as the result of a strict examination of the matter, that the error lies here. It is just the same here as with the motion of the sun: In its case it was our eyes that were wrong; in the matter of the concepts above mentioned it is our language itself that pleads most constantly in their favour. In its origin language belongs to an age of the most rudimentary forms of psychology: if we try to conceive of the first conditions of the metaphysics of language, *i.e.*, in plain English, of reason, we immediately find ourselves in the midst of a system of fetichism. For here, the doer and his deed are seen in all circumstances, will is believed in as a cause in general; the ego is taken for granted, the ego as Being, and as substance, and the faith in the ego as substance is projected into all things – in this way, alone, the concept 'thing' is created. Being is thought into and insinuated into everything as cause; from the concept 'ego', alone, can the concept 'Being' proceed. At the beginning stands the tremendously fatal error of supposing the will to be something that actuates, – a faculty. Now we know that it is only a word.* Very much later, in a world a thousand times more enlightened, the assurance, the subjective certitude, in the handling of the categories of reason came into the minds of philosophers as a surprise. They concluded that these categories could not be derived from experience, – on the contrary, the whole of experience rather contradicts them. *Whence do they come therefore*? In India, as in Greece, the same mistake was made: 'we must already once have lived in a higher world (instead of in a much lower one, which would have been the truth!), we must have been divine, for we possess reason!'... Nothing indeed has exercised a more simple power of persuasion hitherto than the error of Being, as it was formulated by the Eleatics for instance: in its favour are every word and every sentence that we utter! – Even the opponents of the Eleatics succumbed to the seductive powers of their concept of Being. Among others there was Democritus in his discovery of the atom. 'Reason' in language! – oh what a deceptive old witch it has been! I fear we shall never be rid of God, so long as we still believe in grammar.

6

People will feel grateful to me if I condense a point of view, which is at once so important and so new, into four theses: by this means I shall facilitate comprehension, and shall likewise challenge contradiction.

Proposition One. The reasons upon which the apparent nature of 'this' world have been based, rather tend to prove its reality, – any other kind of reality defies demonstration.

Proposition Two. The characteristics with which man has endowed the 'true Being' of things, are the characteristics of non-Being, of *nonentity*. The 'true world' has been erected upon a contradiction of the real world; and it is indeed an apparent world, seeing that it is merely a *moralo-optical* delusion.

Proposition Three. There is no sense in spinning yarns about another world, provided, of course, that we do not possess a mighty instinct which urges us to slander, belittle, and cast suspicion upon this life: in this case we should be avenging ourselves on this life with the phantasmagoria of 'another', of a 'better' life.

---

* Nietzsche here refers to the concept 'free will' of the Christians; this does not mean that there is no such thing as will – that is to say a powerful determining force from within. – TR.

Proposition Four. To divide the world into a 'true' and an 'apparent' world, whether after the manner of Christianity or of Kant (after all a Christian in disguise), is only a sign of decadence – a symptom of *degenerating* life. The fact that the artist esteems the appearance of a thing higher than reality, is no objection to this statement. For 'appearance' signifies once more reality here, but in a selected, strengthened and corrected form. The tragic artist is no pessimist – he says Yea to everything questionable and terrible, he is Dionysian.

HOW THE 'TRUE WORLD' ULTIMATELY BECAME A FABLE

THE HISTORY OF AN ERROR

1. The true world, attainable to the sage, the pious man and the man of virtue, – he lives in it, *he is it*.
    (The most ancient form of the idea was relatively clever, simple, convincing. It was a paraphrase of the proposition 'I, Plato, am the truth.')

2. The true world which is unattainable for the moment, is promised to the sage, to the pious man and to the man of virtue ('to the sinner who repents').
    (Progress of the idea: it becomes more subtle, more insidious, more evasive, – *It becomes a woman*, it becomes Christian.)

3. The true world is unattainable, it cannot be proved, it cannot promise anything; but even as a thought, alone, it is a comfort, an obligation, a command.
    (At bottom this is still the old sun; but seen through mist and scepticism: the idea has become sublime, pale, northern, Königsbergian.)*

4. The true world – is it unattainable? At all events it is unattained. And as unattained it is also *unknown*. Consequently it no longer comforts, nor saves, nor constrains: what could something unknown constrain us to?
    (The grey of dawn. Reason stretches itself and yawns for the first time. The cock-crow of positivism.)

---

* Kant was a native of Königsberg and lived there all his life. Did Nietzsche know that Kant was simply a Scotch Puritan, whose family had settled in Germany?

5. The 'true world' – an idea that no longer serves any purpose, that no longer constrains one to anything, – a useless idea that has become quite superfluous, consequently an exploded idea: let us abolish it!

> (Bright daylight; breakfast; the return of common sense and of cheerfulness; Plato blushes for shame and all free-spirits kick up a shindy.)

6. We have suppressed the true world: what world survives? The apparent world perhaps?... Certainly not! *In abolishing the true world we have also abolished the world of appearance!*

> (Noon; the moment of the shortest shadows; the end of the longest error; mankind's zenith; *Incipit Zarathustra*.)

MORALITY AS THE ENEMY OF NATURE

1

There is a time when all passions are simply fatal in their action, when they wreck their victims with the weight of their folly, – and there is a later period, a very much later period, when they marry with the spirit, when they 'spiritualise' themselves. Formerly, owing to the stupidity inherent in passion, men waged war against passion itself: men pledged themselves to annihilate it, – all ancient moral-mongers were unanimous on this point, '*il faut tuer les passions*'. The most famous formula for this stands in the New Testament, in that Sermon on the Mount, where, let it be said incidentally, things are by no means regarded *from a height*. It is said there, for instance, with an application to sexuality: 'if thy eye offend thee, pluck it out': fortunately no Christian acts in obedience to this precept. To annihilate the passions and desires, simply on account of their stupidity, and to obviate the unpleasant consequences of their stupidity, seems to us today merely an aggravated form of stupidity. We no longer admire those dentists who extract teeth simply in order that they may not ache again. On the other hand, it will be admitted with some reason, that on the soil from which Christianity grew, the idea of the 'spiritualisation of passion' could not possibly have been conceived. The early Church, as everyone knows, certainly did wage war against the 'intelligent', in favour of the 'poor in spirit'. In these circumstances how could the passions be combated intelligently? The Church combats passion by means of excision of all kinds: its practice, its 'remedy', is *castration*. It never inquires 'how can a desire be spiritualised, beautified, deified?' In all ages it has laid the weight of discipline in the process of extirpation (the extirpation of sensuality, pride, lust of dominion, lust of property, and revenge). – But to attack the passions at their roots, means attacking life itself at its source: the method of the Church is hostile to life.

2

The same means, castration and extirpation, are instinctively chosen for waging war against a passion, by those who are too weak of will, too degenerate, to impose some sort of moderation upon it; by those natures who, to speak in metaphor (and without metaphor), need *la Trappe*, or some kind of ultimatum of war, a *gulf* set between themselves and a passion. Only degenerates find radical methods indispensable: weakness of will, or more strictly speaking, the inability not to react to a stimulus, is in itself simply another form of degeneracy. Radical and mortal hostility to sensuality, remains a suspicious symptom: it justifies one in being suspicious of the general state of one who goes to such extremes. Moreover, that hostility and hatred reach their height only when such natures no longer possess enough strength of character to adopt the radical remedy, to renounce their inner 'Satan'. Look at the whole history of the priests, the philosophers, and the artists as well: the most poisonous diatribes against the senses have not been said by the impotent, nor by the ascetics; but by those impossible ascetics, by those who found it necessary to be ascetics.

3

The spiritualisation of sensuality is called *love*: it is a great triumph over Christianity. Another triumph is our spiritualisation of hostility. It consists in the fact that we are beginning to realise very profoundly the value of having enemies: in short that with them we are forced to do and to conclude precisely the reverse of what we previously did and concluded. In all ages the Church wished to annihilate its enemies: we, the immoralists and Antichrists, see our advantage in the survival of the Church. Even in political life, hostility has now become more spiritual – much more cautious, much more thoughtful, and much more moderate. Almost every party sees its self-preservative interests in preventing the Opposition from going to pieces; and the same applies to politics on a grand scale. A new creation, more particularly, like the new Empire, has more need of enemies than friends: only as a contrast does it begin to feel necessary, only as a contrast does it *become* necessary. And we behave in precisely the same way to the 'inner enemy': in this quarter too we have spiritualised enmity, in this quarter too we have understood its value. A man is productive only in so far as he is rich in contrasted instincts; he can remain young only on condition that his soul does not begin to take things easy and to yearn for peace. Nothing has grown more alien to us than that old desire – the 'peace of the soul', which is the aim of Christianity. Nothing could make us less envious than the moral cow and the plump happiness of a clean conscience. The man who has renounced war has renounced a grand life. In many cases, of course, 'peace of the soul' is merely a misunderstanding, it is something *very different* which has failed to find a more honest name for itself. Without either circumlocution or prejudice I will suggest a few cases. 'Peace of the soul' may for instance be the sweet effulgence of rich animality in the realm of morality (or religion). Or the first presage of weariness, the first shadow that evening, every kind of evening, is wont to cast. Or a sign that the air is moist, and that winds are blowing up from the south. Or unconscious gratitude for a good digestion (sometimes called 'brotherly love'). Or the serenity of the convalescent, on whose lips all things have a new taste, and who bides his time. Or the condition which follows upon a thorough gratification of our strongest passion, the well-being of unaccustomed satiety. Or the senility of our will, of our desires, and of our vices. Or laziness, coaxed by vanity into togging itself out in a moral garb. Or the ending of a state of long suspense and of agonising uncertainty, by a state of certainty, of even terrible certainty. Or the expression of ripeness and mastery in the midst of a task, of a creative work, of a production, of a thing willed, the calm breathing that denotes that 'freedom of will' has been attained. Who knows? – maybe the *Twilight of the Idols* is only a sort of 'peace of the soul'.

4

I will formulate a principle. All naturalism in morality – that is to say, every sound morality is ruled by a life instinct, – any one of the laws of life is fulfilled by the definite canon 'thou shalt'; 'thou shalt not' and any sort of obstacle or hostile element in the road of life is thus cleared away. Conversely, the morality which is antagonistic to nature – that is to say, almost every morality that has been taught, honoured and preached hitherto, is directed precisely against the life-instincts, – it is a condemnation, now secret, now blatant and impudent, of these very instincts. Inasmuch as it says 'God sees into the heart of man,' it says Nay to the profoundest and most superior desires of life and takes God as the enemy of life. The saint in whom God is well pleased, is the ideal eunuch. Life terminates where the 'Kingdom of God' begins.

5

Admitting that you have understood the villainy of such a mutiny against life as that which has become almost sacrosanct in Christian morality, you have fortunately understood something besides; and that is the futility, the fictitiousness, the absurdity and the falseness of such a mutiny. For the condemnation of life by a living creature is after all but the symptom of a definite kind of life: the question as to whether the condemnation is justified or the reverse is not even raised. In order even to approach the problem of the value of life, a man would need to be placed outside life, and moreover know it as well as one, as many, as all in fact, who have lived it. These are reasons enough to prove to us that this problem is an inaccessible one to us. When we speak of values, we speak under the inspiration, and through the optics of life: life itself urges us to determine values: life itself values through us when we determine values. From which it follows that even that morality which is antagonistic to life, and which conceives God as the opposite and the condemnation of life, is only a valuation of life – of what life? of what kind of life? But I have already answered this question: it is the valuation of declining, of enfeebled, of exhausted and of condemned life. Morality, as it has been understood hitherto – as it was finally formulated by Schopenhauer in the words 'The Denial of the Will to Life', is the instinct of degeneration itself, which converts itself into an imperative: it says: 'Perish!' It is the death sentence of men who are already doomed.

6

Let us at last consider how exceedingly simple it is on our part to say: 'Man should be thus and thus!' Reality shows us a marvellous wealth of types, and a luxuriant variety of forms and changes: and yet the first wretch of a moral loafer that comes along cries 'No! Man should be different!' He even knows what man should be like, does this sanctimonious prig: he draws his own face on the wall and declares: '*ecce homo!*' But even when the moralist addresses himself only to the individual and says 'thus and thus shouldst thou be!' he still makes an ass of himself. The individual in his past and future is a piece of fate, one law the more, one necessity the more for all that is to come and is to be. To say to him 'change thyself', is tantamount to saying that everything should change, even backwards as well. Truly these have been consistent moralists, they wished man to be different, *i.e.*, virtuous; they wished him to be after their own image – that is to say sanctimonious humbugs. And to this end they denied the world! No slight form of insanity! No modest form of immodesty! Morality, in so far it condemns *per se*, and *not* out of any aim, consideration or motive of life, is a specific error, for which no one should feel any mercy, a degenerate idiosyncrasy, that has done an unutterable amount of harm. We others, we immoralists, on the contrary, have opened our hearts wide to all kinds of comprehension, understanding and approbation.* We do not deny readily, we glory in saying yea to things. Our eyes have opened ever wider and wider to that economy which still employs and knows how to use to its own advantage all that which the sacred craziness of priests and the morbid reason in priests, rejects; to that economy in the law of life which draws its own advantage even out of the repulsive race of bigots, the priests and the virtuous, – what advantage? But we ourselves, we immoralists, are the reply to this question.

---

*   *Cf.* Spinoza, who says in the *Tractatus politico* (1677), Chap. I, § 4: '*Sedulo curavi, humanas actiones non ridere, non tugert, negue detestari, sed intelligere*' ('I have carefully endeavoured not to deride, or deplore, or detest human actions, but to understand them.'). – TR.

THE FOUR GREAT ERRORS

1

The error of the confusion of cause and effect. – There is no more dangerous error than to confound the effect with the cause: I call this error the intrinsic perversion of reason. Nevertheless this error is one of the most ancient and most recent habits of mankind. In one part of the world it has even been canonised; and it bears the name of 'Religion' and 'Morality'. Every postulate formulated by religion and morality contains it. Priests and the promulgators of moral laws are the promoters of this perversion of reason. – Let me give you an example. Everybody knows the book of the famous Cornaro, in which he recommends his slender diet as the recipe for a long, happy and also virtuous life. Few books have been so widely read, and to this day many thousand copies of it are still printed annually in England. I do not doubt that there is scarcely a single book (the Bible of course excepted) that has worked more mischief, shortened more lives, than this well-meant curiosity. The reason of this is the confusion of effect and cause. This worthy Italian saw the cause of his long life in his diet: whereas the prerequisites of long life, which are exceptional slowness of molecular change, and a low rate of expenditure in energy, were the cause of his meagre diet. He was not at liberty to eat a small or a great amount. His frugality was not the result of free choice, he would have been ill had he eaten more. He who does not happen to be a carp, however, is not only wise to eat well, but is also compelled to do so. A scholar of the present day, with his rapid consumption of nervous energy, would soon go to the dogs on Cornaro's diet. *Crede experto.*

2

The most general principle lying at the root of every religion and morality, is this: 'Do this and that and avoid this and that – and thou wilt be happy. Otherwise –.' Every morality and every religion is this Imperative – I call it the great original sin of reason, – *immortal unreason*. In my mouth this principle is converted into its opposite – first example of my 'Transvaluation of all Values': a well-constituted man, a man who is one of 'Nature's lucky strokes', *must* perform certain actions and instinctively fear other actions; he introduces the element of order, of which he is the physiological manifestation, into his relations with men and things. In a formula: his virtue is the consequence of his good constitution. Longevity and plentiful offspring are not the reward of virtue, virtue itself is on the contrary that retardation of the metabolic process which, among other things, results in a long life and in plentiful offspring, in short in *Cornarism*. The Church and morality say: 'A race, a people perish through vice and luxury.' My reinstated reason says: when a people are going to the dogs, when they are degenerating physiologically, vice and luxury (that is to say, the need of ever stronger and more frequent stimuli such as all exhausted natures are acquainted with) are bound to result. Such and such a young man grows pale and withered prematurely. His friends say this or that illness is the cause of it I say: the fact that he became ill, the fact that he did not resist illness, was in itself already the outcome of impoverished life, of hereditary exhaustion. The newspaper reader says: such and such a party by committing such an error will meet its death. My superior politics say: a party that can make such mistakes, is in its last agony – it no longer possesses any certainty of instinct. Every mistake is in every sense the sequel to degeneration of the instincts, to disintegration of the will. This is almost the definition of evil, Everything valuable is instinct – and consequently easy, necessary, free. Exertion is an objection, the god is characteristically different from the hero (in my language: light feet are the first attribute of divinity).

3

The error of false causality. In all ages men have believed that they knew what a cause was: but whence did we derive this knowledge, or more accurately, this faith in the fact that we know? Out of the realm of the famous 'inner facts of consciousness', not one of which has yet proved itself to be a fact. We believed ourselves to be causes even in the action of the will; we thought that in this matter at least we caught causality red-handed. No one doubted that all the *antecedentia* of an action were to be sought in consciousness, and could be discovered there – as 'motive' – if only they were sought. Otherwise we should not be free to perform them, we should not have been responsible for them. Finally who would have questioned that a thought is caused?

that the ego causes the thought? Of these three 'facts of inner consciousness' by means of which causality seemed to be guaranteed, the first and most convincing is that of the will as cause; the conception of consciousness ('spirit') as a cause, and subsequently that of the ego (the 'subject') as a cause, were merely born afterwards, once the causality of the will stood established as 'given', as a fact of experience. Meanwhile we have come to our senses. Today we no longer believe a word of all this. The 'inner world' is full of phantoms and will-o'-the-wisps: the will is one of these. The will no longer actuates, consequently it no longer explains anything – all it does is to accompany processes; it may even be absent. The so-called 'motive' is another error. It is merely a ripple on the surface of consciousness, a side issue of the action, which is much more likely to conceal than to reveal the *antecedentia* of the latter. And as for the ego! It has become legendary, fictional, a play upon words: it has ceased utterly and completely from thinking, feeling, and willing! What is the result of it all? There are no such things as spiritual causes. The whole of popular experience on this subject went to the devil! That is the result of it all. For we had blissfully abused that experience, we had built the world upon it as a world of causes, as a world of will, as a world of spirit. The most antiquated and most traditional psychology has been at work here, it has done nothing else: all phenomena were deeds in the light of this psychology, and all deeds were the result of will; according to it the world was a complex mechanism of agents, an agent (a 'subject') lay at the root of all things. Man projected his three 'inner facts of consciousness', the will, the spirit, and the ego in which he believed most firmly, outside himself. He first deduced the concept Being out of the concept Ego, he supposed 'things' to exist as he did himself, according to his notion of the ego as cause. Was it to be wondered at that later on he always found in things only that which he had laid in them? – The thing itself, I repeat, the concept thing was merely a reflex of the belief in the ego as cause. And even your atom, my dear good Mechanists and Physicists, what an amount of error, of rudimentary psychology still adheres to it! – Not to speak of the 'thing-in-itself', of the *horrendum pudendum* of the metaphysicians! The error of spirit regarded as a cause, confounded with reality! And made the measure of reality! And called *God*!

4

The error of imaginary causes. Starting out from dreamland, we find that to any definite sensation, like that produced by a distant cannon shot for instance, we are wont to ascribe a cause after the fact (very often quite a little romance in which the dreamer himself is, of course, the hero). Meanwhile the sensation becomes protracted like a sort of continuous echo, until, as it were, the instinct of causality allows it to come to the front rank, no longer however as a chance occurrence, but as a thing which has some meaning. The cannon shot presents itself in a *causal* manner, by means of an apparent reversal in the order of time. That which occurs last, the motivation, is experienced first, often with a hundred details which flash past like lightning, and the shot is the *result*. What has happened? The ideas suggested by a particular state of our senses, are misinterpreted as the cause of that state. As a matter of fact we proceed in precisely the same manner when we are awake. The greater number of our general sensations – every kind of obstacle, pressure, tension, explosion in the interplay of the organs, and more particularly the condition of the *nervus sympathicus* – stimulate our instinct of causality: we will have a reason which will account for our feeling thus or thus, – for feeling ill or well. We are never satisfied by merely ascertaining the fact that we feel thus or thus: we admit this fact – we become conscious of it – only when we have attributed it to some kind of motivation. Memory, which, in such circumstances unconsciously becomes active, adduces former conditions of a like kind, together with the causal interpretations with which they are associated, – but not their real cause. The belief that the ideas, the accompanying processes of consciousness, have been the causes, is certainly produced by the agency of memory. And in this way we become *accustomed* to a particular interpretation of causes which, truth to tell, actually hinders and even utterly prevents the investigation of the proper cause.

5

The psychological explanation of the above fact. To trace something unfamiliar back to something familiar, is at once a relief, a comfort and a satisfaction, while it also produces a feeling of power. The unfamiliar involves danger, anxiety and care – the fundamental instinct is to get rid of these painful circumstances. First principle: any explanation is better than none at all. Since, at bottom, it is only a question of shaking one's self free from certain oppressive ideas, the means employed to this end are not selected with overmuch punctiliousness: the first idea by means of which the unfamiliar is revealed as familiar, produces a feeling of such comfort that it is 'held to be true'. The proof of happiness ('of power') as the criterion of truth. The instinct of causality is therefore conditioned and stimulated by the feeling of fear. Whenever possible, the question 'why?' should not only educe the cause as cause, but rather a certain kind of cause – a comforting, liberating and reassuring cause. The first result of this need is that something known or already experienced, and recorded in the memory, is posited as the cause. The new factor, that which has not been experienced and which is unfamiliar, is excluded from the sphere of causes. Not only do we try to find a certain kind of explanation as the cause, but those kinds of explanations are selected and preferred which dissipate most rapidly the sensation of strangeness, novelty and unfamiliarity – in fact the most ordinary explanations. And the result is that a certain manner of postulating causes tends to predominate ever more and more, becomes concentrated into a system, and finally reigns supreme, to the complete exclusion of all other causes and explanations. The banker thinks immediately of business, the Christian of 'sin', and the girl of her love affair.

6

The whole domain of morality and religion may be classified under the rubric 'imaginary causes'. The 'explanation' of general unpleasant sensations. These sensations are dependent upon certain creatures who are hostile to us (evil spirits: the most famous example of this – the mistaking of hysterical women for witches). These sensations are dependent upon actions which are reprehensible (the feeling of 'sin', 'sinfulness' is a manner of accounting for a certain physiological disorder – people always find reasons for being dissatisfied with themselves). These sensations depend upon punishment, upon compensation for something which we ought not to have done, which we ought not to have been (this idea was generalised in a more impudent form by Schopenhauer, into that principle in which morality appears in its real colours – that is to say, as a veritable poisoner and slanderer of life: 'all great suffering, whether mental or physical, reveals what we deserve: for it could not visit us if we did not deserve it,' – *The World as Will and Idea*, vol. 2, p. 666). These sensations are the outcome of ill-considered actions, having evil consequences, (the passions, the senses, postulated as causes, as guilty. By means of other calamities distressing physiological conditions are interpreted as 'merited'). – The 'explanation' of pleasant sensations. These sensations are dependent upon a trust in God. They may depend upon our consciousness of having done one or two good actions (a so-called 'good conscience' is a physiological condition, which may be the outcome of good digestion). They may depend upon the happy issue of certain undertakings (an ingenuous mistake: the happy issue of an undertaking certainly does not give a hypochondriac or a Pascal any general sensation of pleasure). They may depend upon faith, love and hope, – the Christian virtues. As a matter of fact all these pretended explanations are but the results of certain states, and as it were translations of feelings of pleasure and pain into a false dialect: a man is in a condition of hopefulness because the dominant physiological sensation of his being is again one of strength and wealth; he trusts in God because the feeling of abundance and power gives him a peaceful state of mind. Morality and religion are completely and utterly parts of the psychology of error: in every particular case cause and effect are confounded; as truth is confounded with the effect of that which is believed to be true; or a certain state of consciousness is confounded with the chain of causes which brought it about.

7

The error of free-will. At present we no longer have any mercy upon the concept 'free-will': we know only too well what it is – the most egregious theological trick that has ever existed for the purpose of making mankind 'responsible' in a theological manner, – that is to say, to make mankind dependent upon theologians. I will now explain to you only the psychology of the whole process of inculcating the sense of responsibility. Wherever men try to trace responsibility home to anyone, it is the instinct of punishment and of the desire to judge which is active. Becoming is robbed of its innocence when any particular condition of things is traced to a will, to intentions and to responsible actions. The doctrine of the will was invented principally for the purpose of punishment, – that is to say, with the intention of tracing guilt. The whole of ancient psychology, or the psychology of the will, is the outcome of the fact that its originators, who were the priests at the head of ancient communities, wanted to create for themselves a right to administer punishments – or the right for God to do so. Men were thought of as 'free' in order that they might be judged and punished – in order that they might be held guilty: consequently every action had to be regarded as voluntary, and the origin of every action had to be imagined as lying in consciousness (in this way the most fundamentally fraudulent character of psychology was established as the very principle of psychology itself). Now that we have entered upon the opposite movement, now that we immoralists are trying with all our power to eliminate the concepts of guilt and punishment from the world once more, and to cleanse psychology, history, nature and all social institutions and customs of all signs of those two concepts, we recognise no more radical opponents than the theologians, who with their notion of 'a moral order of things', still continue to pollute the innocence of Becoming with punishment and guilt. Christianity is the metaphysics of the hangman.

8

What then, alone, can our teaching be? – That no one gives man his qualities, neither God, society, his parents, his ancestors, nor himself (this nonsensical idea which is at last refuted here, was taught as 'intelligible freedom' by Kant, and perhaps even as early as Plato himself). No one is responsible for the fact that he exists at all, that he is constituted as he is, and that he happens to be in certain circumstances and in a particular environment. The fatality of his being cannot be divorced from the fatality of all that which has been and will be. This is not the result of an individual intention, of a will, of an aim, there is no attempt at attaining to any 'ideal man', or 'ideal happiness' or 'ideal morality' with him – it is absurd to wish him to be careering towards some sort of purpose. *We* invented the concept 'purpose'; in reality purpose is altogether lacking. One is necessary, one is a piece of fate, one belongs to the whole, one is in the whole, – there is nothing that could judge, measure, compare, and condemn our existence, for that would mean judging, measuring, comparing and condemning the whole. *But there is nothing outside the whole!* The fact that no one shall any longer be made responsible, that the nature of existence may not be traced to a *causa prima*, that the world is an entity neither as a sensorium nor as a spirit – *this alone is the great deliverance* – thus alone is the innocence of Becoming restored…. The concept 'God' has been the greatest objection to existence hitherto…. We deny God, we deny responsibility in God: thus alone do we save the world.

THE 'IMPROVERS' OF MANKIND

1

You are aware of my demand upon philosophers, that they should take up a stand Beyond Good and Evil, – that they should have the illusion of the moral judgment beneath them. This demand is the result of a point of view which I was the first to formulate: *that there are no such things as moral facts.* Moral judgment has this in common with the religious one, that it believes in realities which are not real. Morality is only an interpretation of certain phenomena: or, more strictly speaking, a misinterpretation of them. Moral judgment, like the religious one, belongs to a stage of ignorance in which even the concept of reality, the distinction between real and imagined things, is still lacking: so that truth, at such a stage, is applied to a host of things which today we call 'imaginary'. That is why the moral judgment must never be taken quite literally: as such it is sheer nonsense. As a sign code, however, it is invaluable: to him at least who knows, it reveals the most valuable facts concerning cultures and inner conditions, which did not know enough to 'understand' themselves. Morality is merely a sign-language, simply symptomatology: one must already know what it is all about in order to turn it to any use.

2

Let me give you one example, quite provisionally. In all ages there have been people who wished to 'improve' mankind: this above all is what was called morality. But the most different tendencies are concealed beneath the same word. Both the taming of the beast man, and the rearing of a particular type of man, have been called 'improvement': these zoological *termini*, alone, represent real things – real things of which the typical 'improver', the priest, naturally knows nothing, and will know nothing. To call the taming of an animal 'improving' it, sounds to our ears almost like a joke. He who knows what goes on in menageries, doubts very much whether an animal is improved in such places. It is certainly weakened, it is made less dangerous, and by means of the depressing influence of fear, pain, wounds, and hunger, it is converted into a sick animal. And the same holds good of the tamed man whom the priest has 'improved'. In the early years of the Middle Ages, during which the Church was most distinctly and above all a menagerie, the most beautiful examples of the 'blond beast' were hunted down in all directions, – the noble Germans, for instance, were 'improved'. But what did this 'improved' German, who had been lured to the monastery look like after the process? He looked like a caricature of man, like an abortion: he had become a 'sinner', he was caged up, he had been imprisoned behind a host of appalling notions. He now lay there, sick, wretched, malevolent even toward himself: full of hate for the instincts of life, full of suspicion in regard to all that is still strong and happy. In short a 'Christian'. In physiological terms: in a fight with an animal, the only way of making it weak may be to make it sick. The Church understood this: it ruined man, it made him weak, – but it laid claim to having 'improved' him.

3

Now let us consider the other case which is called morality, the case of the rearing of a particular race and species. The most magnificent example of this is offered by Indian morality, and is sanctioned religiously as the 'Law of Manu'. In this book the task is set of rearing no less than four races at once: a priestly race, a warrior race, a merchant and agricultural race, and finally a race of servants – the Sudras. It is quite obvious that we are no longer in a circus watching tamers of wild animals in this book. To have conceived even the plan of such a breeding scheme, presupposes the existence of a man who is a hundred times milder and more reasonable than the mere lion-tamer. One breathes more freely, after stepping out of the Christian atmosphere of hospitals and prisons, into this more salubrious, loftier and more spacious world. What a wretched thing the New Testament is beside Manu, what an evil odour hangs around it! – But even this organisation found it necessary to be terrible, – not this time in a struggle with the animal-man, but with his opposite, the non-caste man, the hotch-potch man, the Chandala. And once again it had no other means of making him weak and harmless, than by making him sick, – it was the struggle with the greatest 'number'. Nothing perhaps is more offensive to our feelings than these measures of security on the part of Indian morality. The third edict, for instance (Avadana-Sastra I.), which treats 'of impure vegetables', ordains that the only nourishment that the Chandala should be allowed must consist of garlic and onions, as the holy scriptures forbid their being given corn or grain-bearing fruit, water and fire. The same edict declares that the water which they need must be drawn neither out of rivers, wells or ponds, but only out of the ditches leading to swamps and out of the holes left by the footprints of animals. They are likewise forbidden to wash either their linen or themselves since the water which is graciously granted to them must only be used for quenching their thirst. Finally Sudra women are forbidden to assist Chandala women at their confinements, while Chandala women are also forbidden to assist each other at such times. The results of sanitary regulations of this kind could not fail to make themselves felt; deadly epidemics and the most ghastly venereal diseases soon appeared, and in consequence of these again 'the law of the knife', that is to say circumcision, was prescribed for male children and the removal of the small labia from the females. Manu himself says: 'the Chandala are the fruit of adultery, incest, and crime (this is the necessary consequence of the idea of breeding). Their clothes shall consist only of the rags torn from corpses, their vessels shall be the fragments of broken pottery, their ornaments shall be made of old iron, and their religion shall be the worship of evil spirits; without rest they shall wander from place to place. They are forbidden to write from left to right or to use their right hand in writing: the use of the right hand and writing from left to right are reserved to people of virtue, to people of race.'

4

These regulations are instructive enough: we can see in them the absolutely pure and primeval humanity of the Aryans, – we learn that the notion 'pure blood', is the reverse of harmless. On the other hand it becomes clear among which people the hatred, the Chandala hatred of this humanity has been immortalised, among which people it has become religion and genius. From this point of view the gospels are documents of the highest value; and the Book of Enoch is still more so. Christianity as sprung from Jewish roots and comprehensible only as grown upon this soil, represents the counter-movement against that morality of breeding, of race and of privilege: – it is essentially an anti-Aryan religion: Christianity is the transvaluation of all Aryan values, the triumph of Chandala values, the proclaimed gospel of the poor and of the low, the general insurrection of all the down-trodden, the wretched, the bungled and the botched, against the 'race', – the immortal revenge of the Chandala as the *religion of love*.

5

The morality of breeding and the morality of taming, in the means which they adopt in order to prevail, are quite worthy of each other: we may lay down as a leading principle that in order to create morality a man must have the absolute will to immorality. This is the great and strange problem with which I have so long been occupied: the psychology of the 'improvers' of mankind. A small, and at bottom perfectly insignificant fact, known as the *pia fraus*, first gave me access to this problem: the *pia fraus*, the heirloom of all philosophers and priests who 'improve' mankind. Neither Manu, nor Plato, nor Confucius, nor the teachers of Judaism and Christianity, have ever doubted their right to falsehood. They have never doubted their right to quite a number of other things. To express oneself in a formula, one might say: – all means which have been used heretofore with the object of making man moral, were through and through immoral.

THINGS THE GERMANS LACK

1

Among Germans at the present day it does not suffice to have intellect; one is actually forced to appropriate it, to lay claim to it.

Maybe I know the Germans, perhaps I may tell them a few home-truths. Modern Germany represents such an enormous store of inherited and acquired capacity, that for some time it might spend this accumulated treasure even with some prodigality. It is no superior culture that has ultimately become prevalent with this modern tendency, nor is it by any means delicate taste, or noble beauty of the instincts; but rather a number of virtues more manly than any that other European countries can show. An amount of good spirits and self-respect, plenty of firmness in human relations and in the reciprocity of duties; much industry and much perseverance – and a certain inherited soberness which is much more in need of a spur than of a brake. Let me add that in this country people still obey without feeling that obedience humiliates. And no one despises his opponent.

You observe that it is my desire to be fair to the Germans: and in this respect I should not like to be untrue to myself, – I must therefore also state my objections to them. It costs a good deal to attain to a position of power; for power *stultifies*. The Germans – they were once called a people of thinkers: do they really think at all at present? Nowadays the Germans are bored by intellect, they mistrust intellect; politics have swallowed up all earnestness for really intellectual things – 'Germany, Germany above all'.* I fear this was the death-blow to German philosophy. 'Are there any German philosophers? Are there any German poets? Are there any good German books?' people ask me abroad. I blush; but with that pluck which is peculiar to me, even in moments of desperation, I reply: 'Yes, Bismarck!' – Could I have dared to confess what books *are* read today? Cursed instinct of mediocrity!

---

* The German national hymn: 'Deutschland, Deutschland über alles.' – TR.

2

What might not German intellect have been! – who has not thought sadly upon this question! But this nation has deliberately stultified itself for almost a thousand years: nowhere else have the two great European narcotics, alcohol and Christianity, been so viciously abused as in Germany. Recently a third opiate was added to the list, one which in itself alone would have sufficed to complete the ruin of all subtle and daring intellectual animation, I speak of music, our costive and constipating German music. How much peevish ponderousness, paralysis, dampness, dressing-gown languor, and beer is there not in German intelligence!

How is it really possible that young men who consecrate their whole lives to the pursuit of intellectual ends, should not feel within them the first instinct of intellectuality, the *self-preservative instinct of the intellect* – and should drink beer? The alcoholism of learned youths does not incapacitate them for becoming scholars – a man quite devoid of intellect may be a great scholar – but it is a problem in every other respect. Where can that soft degeneracy not be found, which is produced in the intellect by beer! I once laid my finger upon a case of this sort, which became almost famous – the degeneration of our leading German free-spirit, the *clever* David Strauss, into the author of a suburban gospel and New Faith. Not in vain had he sung the praises of 'the dear old brown liquor' in verse – true unto death.

3

I have spoken of German intellect. I have said that it is becoming coarser and shallower. Is that enough? – In reality something very different frightens me, and that is the ever steady decline of German earnestness, German profundity, and German passion in things intellectual. Not only intellectuality, but also pathos has altered. From time to time I come in touch with German universities; what an extraordinary atmosphere prevails among their scholars! what barrenness! and what self-satisfied and lukewarm intellectuality! For anyone to point to German science as an argument against me would show that he grossly misunderstood my meaning, while it would also prove that he had not read a word of my writings. For seventeen years I have done little else than expose the de-intellectualising influence of our modern scientific studies. The severe slavery to which every individual nowadays is condemned by the enormous range covered by the sciences, is the chief reason why fuller, richer and profounder natures can find no education or educators that are fit for them. Nothing is more deleterious to this age than the superfluity of pretentious loafers and fragmentary human beings; our universities are really the involuntary forcing houses for this kind of withering-up of the instincts of intellectuality. And the whole of Europe is beginning to know this – politics on a large scale deceive no one. Germany is becoming ever more and more the Flat-land of Europe. I am still in search of a German with whom I could be serious after my own fashion. And how much more am I in search of one with whom I could be cheerful – *Twilight of the Idols*: ah! what man today would be capable of understanding the kind of seriousness from which a philosopher is recovering in this work! It is our cheerfulness that people understand least.

4

Let us examine another aspect of the question: it is not only obvious that German culture is declining, but adequate reasons for this decline are not lacking. After all, nobody can spend more than he has: – this is true of individuals, it is also true of nations. If you spend your strength in acquiring power, or in politics on a large scale, or in economy, or in universal commerce, or in parliamentarism, or in military interests – if you dissipate the modicum of reason, of earnestness, of will, and of self-control that constitutes your nature in one particular fashion, you cannot dissipate it in another. Culture and the state – let no one be deceived on this point – are antagonists: A 'culture-state'* is merely a modern idea. The one lives upon the other, the one flourishes at the expense of the other. All great periods of culture have been periods of political decline; that which is great from the standpoint of culture, was always unpolitical – even anti-political. Goethe's heart opened at the coming of Napoleon – it closed at the thought of the 'Wars of Liberation'. At the very moment when Germany arose as a great power in the world of politics, France won new importance as a force in the world of culture. Even at this moment a large amount of fresh intellectual earnestness and passion has emigrated to Paris; the question of pessimism, for instance, and the question of Wagner; in France almost all psychological and artistic questions are considered with incomparably

---

* The word *Kultur-Staat* 'culture-state' has become a standard expression in the German language, and is applied to the leading European States. – TR.

more subtlety and thoroughness than they are in Germany – the Germans are even incapable of this kind of earnestness. In the history of European culture the rise of the Empire signifies, above all, a displacement of the centre of gravity. Everywhere people are already aware of this: in things that really matter – and these after all constitute culture – the Germans are no longer worth considering. I ask you, can you show me one single man of brains who could be mentioned in the same breath with other European thinkers, like your Goethe, your Hegel, your Heinrich Heine, and your Schopenhauer? – The fact that there is no longer a single German philosopher worth mentioning is an increasing wonder.

5

Everything that matters has been lost sight of by the whole of the higher educational system of Germany: the end quite as much as the means to that end. People forget that education, the process of cultivation itself, is the end – and not 'the Empire' – they forget that the *educator* is required for this end – and not the public-school teacher and university scholar. Educators are needed who are themselves educated, superior and noble intellects, who can prove that they are thus qualified, that they are ripe and mellow products of culture at every moment of their lives, in word and in gesture; – not the learned louts who, like 'superior wet-nurses', are now thrust upon the youth of the land by public schools and universities. With but rare exceptions, that which is lacking in Germany is the first prerequisite of education – that is to say, the educators; hence the decline of German culture. One of those rarest exceptions is my highly respected friend Jacob Burckhardt of Basle: to him above all is Basle indebted for its foremost position in human culture. What the higher schools of Germany really do accomplish is this, they brutally train a vast crowd of young men, in the smallest amount of time possible, to become useful and exploitable servants of the state. 'Higher education' and a vast crowd – these terms contradict each other from the start. All superior education can only concern the exception: a man must be privileged in order to have a right to such a great privilege. All great and beautiful things cannot be a common possession: *pulchrum est paucorum hominum*. – What is it that brings about the decline of German culture? The fact that 'higher education' is no longer a special privilege – the democracy of a process of cultivation that has become 'general', *common*. Nor must it be forgotten that the privileges of the military profession by urging many too many to attend the higher schools, involve the downfall of the latter. In modern Germany nobody is at liberty to give his children a noble education: in regard to their teachers, their curricula, and their educational aims, our higher schools are one and all established upon a fundamentally doubtful mediocre basis. Everywhere, too, a hastiness which is unbecoming rules supreme; just as if something would be forfeited if the young man were not 'finished' at the age of twenty-three, or did not know how to reply to the most essential question, 'which calling to choose?' – The superior kind of man, if you please, does not like 'callings', precisely because he knows himself to be called. He has time, he takes time, he cannot possibly think of becoming 'finished'. – in the matter of higher culture, a man of thirty years is a beginner, a child. Our overcrowded public-schools, our accumulation of foolishly manufactured public-school masters, are a scandal: maybe there are very serious *motives* for defending this state of affairs, as was shown quite recently by the professors of Heidelberg; but there can be no reasons for doing so.

6

In order to be true to my nature, which is affirmative and which concerns itself with contradictions and criticism only indirectly and with reluctance, let me state at once what the three objects are for which we need educators. People must learn to see; they must learn to think, and they must learn to speak and to write: the object of all three of these pursuits is a noble culture. To learn to see – to accustom the eye to calmness, to patience, and to allow things to come up to it; to defer judgment, and to acquire the habit of approaching and grasping an individual case from all sides. This is the first preparatory schooling of intellectuality. One must not respond immediately to a stimulus; one must acquire a command of the obstructing and isolating instincts. To learn to see, as I understand this matter, amounts almost to that which in popular language is called 'strength of will': its essential feature is precisely *not* to *wish* to see, to be able to postpone one's decision. All lack of intellectuality, all vulgarity, arises out of the inability to resist a stimulus: – one must respond or react, every impulse is indulged. In many cases such necessary action is already a sign of morbidity, of decline, and a symptom of exhaustion. Almost everything that coarse popular language characterises as vicious, is merely that physiological inability to refrain from reacting. – As an instance of what it means to have learnt to see, let me state that a man thus trained will as a learner have become generally slow, suspicious, and refractory. With hostile calm he will first allow every kind of strange and *new* thing to come right up to him, – he will draw back his hand at its approach. To stand with all the doors of one's soul wide open, to lie slavishly in the dust before every trivial fact, at all times of the day to be strained ready for the leap, in order to deposit one's self, to plunge one's self, into other souls and other things, in short, the famous 'objectivity' of modern times, is bad taste, it is essentially vulgar and cheap.

7

As to learning how to think – our schools no longer have any notion of such a thing. Even at the universities, among the actual scholars in philosophy, logic as a theory, as a practical pursuit, and as a business, is beginning to die out. Turn to any German book: you will not find the remotest trace of a realisation that there is such a thing as a technique, a plan of study, a will to mastery, in the matter of thinking, – that thinking insists upon being learnt, just as dancing insists upon being learnt, and that thinking insists upon being learnt as a form of dancing. What single German can still say he knows from experience that delicate shudder which *light footfalls* in matters intellectual cause to pervade his whole body and limbs! Stiff awkwardness in intellectual attitudes, and the clumsy fist in grasping – these things are so essentially German, that outside Germany they are absolutely confounded with the German spirit. The German has no fingers for delicate *nuances*. The fact that the people of Germany have actually tolerated their philosophers, more particularly that most deformed cripple of ideas that has ever existed – the great Kant, gives one no inadequate notion of their native elegance. For, truth to tell, dancing in all its forms cannot be excluded from the curriculum of all noble education: dancing with the feet, with ideas, with words, and, need I add that one must also be able to dance with the pen – that one must learn how to write? – But at this stage I should become utterly enigmatical to German readers.

SKIRMISHES IN A WAR
WITH THE AGE

1

My Impossible People. – Seneca, or the toreador of virtue – Rousseau, or the return to nature, in *impuris naturalibus*. – Schiller, or the Moral-Trumpeter of Säckingen. – Dante, or the hyæna that writes poetry in tombs. – Kant, or *cant* as an intelligible character. – Victor Hugo, or the lighthouse on the sea of nonsense. – Liszt, or the school of racing – after women. – George Sand, or *lactea ubertas*, in plain English: the cow with plenty of beautiful milk. – Michelet, or enthusiasm in its shirt sleeves. – Carlyle, or Pessimism after undigested meals. – John Stuart Mill, or offensive lucidity. – The brothers Goncourt, or the two Ajaxes fighting with Homer. Music by Offenbach. – Zola, or the love of stinking.

2

Renan. – Theology, or the corruption of reason by original sin (Christianity). Proof of this, – Renan who, even in those rare cases where he ventures to say either Yes or No on a general question, invariably misses the point with painful regularity. For instance, he would fain associate science and nobility: but surely it must be obvious that science is democratic. He seems to be actuated by a strong desire to represent an aristocracy of intellect: but, at the same time he grovels on his knees, and not only on his knees, before the opposite doctrine, the gospel of the humble. What is the good of all free-spiritedness, modernity, mockery and acrobatic suppleness, if in one's belly one is still a Christian, a Catholic, and even a priest! Renan's forte, precisely like that of a Jesuit and Father Confessor, lies in his seductiveness. His intellectuality is not devoid of that unctuous complacency of a parson, – like all priests, he becomes dangerous only when he loves. He is second to none in the art of skilfully worshipping a dangerous thing. This intellect of Renan's, which in its action is enervating, is one calamity the more, for poor, sick France with her will-power all going to pieces.

3

Sainte-Beuve. – There is naught of man in him; he is full of petty spite towards all virile spirits. He wanders erratically; he is subtle, inquisitive, a little bored, for ever with his ear to keyholes – at bottom a woman, with all woman's revengefulness and sensuality. As a psychologist he is a genius of slander; inexhaustively rich in means to this end; no one understands better than he how to introduce a little poison into praise. In his fundamental instincts he is plebeian and next of kin to Rousseau's resentful spirit: consequently he is a Romanticist – for beneath all romanticism Rousseau's instinct for revenge grunts and frets. He is a revolutionary, but kept within bounds by 'funk'. He is embarrassed in the face of everything that is strong (public opinion, the Academy, the court, even Port Royal). He is embittered against everything great in men and things, against everything that believes in itself. Enough of a poet and of a female to be able to feel greatness as power; he is always turning and twisting, because, like the proverbial worm, he constantly feels that he is being trodden upon. As a critic he has no standard of judgment, no guiding principle, no backbone. Although he possesses the tongue of the Cosmopolitan libertine which can chatter about a thousand things, he has not the courage even to acknowledge his *libertinage*. As a historian he has no philosophy, and lacks the power of philosophical vision, – hence his refusal to act the part of a judge, and his adoption of the mask of 'objectivity' in all important matters. His attitude is better in regard to all those things in which subtle and effete taste is the highest tribunal: in these things he really does have the courage of his own personality – he really does enjoy his own nature – he actually is a *master*, – In some respects he is a prototype of Baudelaire.

4

The Imitation of Christ is one of those books which I cannot even take hold of without physical loathing: it exhales a perfume of the eternally feminine, which to appreciate fully one must be a Frenchman or a Wagnerite. This saint has a way of speaking about love which makes even Parisiennes feel a little curious. – I am told that that *most intelligent* of Jesuits, Auguste Comte, who wished to lead his compatriots back to Rome by the circuitous route of science, drew his inspiration from this book. And I believe it: 'the religion of the heart'.

5

G. Eliot. – They are rid of the Christian God and therefore think it all the more incumbent upon them to hold tight to Christian morality: this is an English way of reasoning; but let us not take it ill in moral females *à la* Eliot. In England, every man who indulges in any trifling emancipation from theology, must retrieve his honour in the most terrifying manner by becoming a moral fanatic. That is how they do penance in that country. – As for us, we act differently. When we renounce the Christian faith, we abandon all right to Christian morality. This is not by any means self-evident and in defiance of English shallow-pates the point must be made ever more and more plain. Christianity is a system, a complete outlook upon the world, conceived as a whole. If its leading concept, the belief in God, is wrenched from it, the whole is destroyed; nothing vital remains in our grasp. Christianity presupposes that man does not and cannot know what is good or bad for him: the Christian believes in God who, alone, can know these things. Christian morality is a command, its origin is transcendental. It is beyond all criticism, all right to criticism; it is true only on condition that God is truth, – it stands or falls with the belief in God. If the English really believe that they know intuitively, and of their own accord, what is good and evil; if, therefore, they assert that they no longer need Christianity as a guarantee of morality, this in itself is simply the outcome of the dominion of Christian valuations, and a proof of the strength and profundity of this dominion. It only shows that the origin of English morality has been forgotten, and that its exceedingly relative right to exist is no longer felt. For Englishmen morality is not yet a problem.

6

George Sand. – I have been reading the first '*Lettres d'un Voyageur*': like everything that springs from Rousseau's influence it is false, made-up, blown out, and exaggerated! I cannot endure this bright wallpaper style, any more than I can bear the vulgar striving after generous feelings. The worst feature about it is certainly the coquettish adoption of male attributes by this female, after the manner of ill-bred schoolboys. And how cold she must have been inwardly all the while, this insufferable artist! She wound herself up like a clock – and wrote. As cold as Hugo and Balzac, as cold as all Romanticists are as soon as they begin to write! And how self-complacently she must have lain there, this prolific ink-yielding cow. For she had something German in her (German in the bad sense), just as Rousseau, her master, had; – something which could only have been possible when French taste was declining! – and Renan adores her!...

7

A Moral for Psychologists. Do not go in for any notebook psychology! Never observe for the sake of observing! Such things lead to a false point of view, to a squint, to something forced and exaggerated. To experience things on purpose – this is not a bit of good. In the midst of an experience a man should not turn his eyes upon himself; in such cases any eye becomes the 'evil eye'. A born psychologist instinctively avoids seeing for the sake of seeing. And the same holds good of the born painter. Such a man never works 'from nature' – he leaves it to his instinct, to his *camera obscura* to sift and to define the 'fact', 'nature', the 'experience'. The general idea, the conclusion, the result, is the only thing that reaches his consciousness. He knows nothing of that wilful process of deducing from particular cases. What is the result when a man sets about this matter differently? – when, for instance, after the manner of Parisian novelists, he goes in for notebook psychology on a large and small scale? Such a man is constantly spying on reality, and every evening he bears home a handful of fresh curios.... But look at the result! – a mass of daubs, at best a piece of mosaic, in any case something heaped together, restless and garish. The Goncourts are the greatest sinners in this respect: they cannot put three sentences together which are not absolutely painful to the eye – the eye of the psychologist. From an artistic standpoint, nature is no model. It exaggerates, distorts, and leaves gaps. Nature is the *accident*. To study 'from nature' seems to me a bad sign: it betrays submission, weakness, fatalism – this lying in the dust before trivial facts is unworthy of a thorough artist. To see *what is* – is the function of another order of intellects, the *anti-artistic*, the matter-of-fact. One must know *who* one is.

8

Concerning the psychology of the artist. For art to be possible at all – that is to say, in order that an æsthetic mode of action and of observation may exist, a certain preliminary physiological state is indispensable *ecstasy*.* This state of ecstasy must first have intensified the susceptibility of the whole machine: otherwise, no art is possible. All kinds of ecstasy, however differently produced, have this power to create art, and above all the state dependent upon sexual excitement – this most venerable and primitive form of ecstasy. The same applies to that ecstasy which is the outcome of all great desires, all strong passions; the ecstasy of the feast, of the arena, of the act of bravery, of victory, of all extreme action; the ecstasy of cruelty; the ecstasy of destruction; the ecstasy following upon certain meteorological influences, as for instance that of spring-time, or upon the use of narcotics; and finally the ecstasy of will, that ecstasy which results from accumulated and surging will-power. – The essential feature of ecstasy is the feeling of increased strength and abundance. Actuated by this feeling a man gives of himself to things, he *forces* them to partake of his riches, he does violence to them – this proceeding is called *idealising*. Let us rid ourselves of a prejudice here: idealising does not consist, as is generally believed, in a suppression or an elimination of detail or of unessential features. A stupendous *accentuation* of the principal characteristics is by far the most decisive factor at work, and in consequence the minor characteristics vanish.

9

In this state a man enriches everything from out his own abundance: what he sees, what he wills, he sees distended, compressed, strong, overladen with power. He transfigures things until they reflect his power, – until they are stamped with his perfection. This compulsion to transfigure into the beautiful is – Art. Everything – even that which he is not, – is nevertheless to such a man a means of rejoicing over himself; in Art man rejoices over himself as perfection. – It is possible to imagine a contrary state, a specifically anti-artistic state of the instincts, – a state in which a man impoverishes, attenuates, and draws the blood from everything. And, truth to tell, history is full of such anti-artists, of such creatures of low vitality who have no choice but

---

*   The German word *Rausch* as used by Nietzsche here, suggests a blend of our two English words 'intoxication' and 'elation'. – TR.

to appropriate everything they see and to suck its blood and make it thinner. This is the case with the genuine Christian, Pascal for instance. There is no such thing as a Christian who is also an artist... Let no one be so childish as to suggest Raphael or any homeopathic Christian of the nineteenth century as an objection to this statement: Raphael said Yea, Raphael *did* Yea, – consequently Raphael was no Christian.

10

What is the meaning of the antithetical concepts *Apollonian* and *Dionysian* which I have introduced into the vocabulary of Æsthetic, as representing two distinct modes of ecstasy? – Apollonian ecstasy acts above all as a force stimulating the eye, so that it acquires the power of vision. The painter, the sculptor, the epic poet are essentially visionaries. In the Dionysian state, on the other hand, the whole system of passions is stimulated and intensified, so that it discharges itself by all the means of expression at once, and vents all its power of representation, of imitation, of transfiguration, of transformation, together with every kind of mimicry and histrionic display at the same time. The essential feature remains the facility in transforming, the inability to refrain from reaction (a similar state to that of certain hysterical patients, who at the slightest hint assume any role). It is impossible for the Dionysian artist not to understand any suggestion; no outward sign of emotion escapes him, he possesses the instinct of comprehension and of divination in the highest degree, just as he is capable of the most perfect art of communication. He enters into every skin, into every passion: he is continually changing himself. Music as we understand it today is likewise a general excitation and discharge of the emotions; but, notwithstanding this, it is only the remnant of a much richer world of emotional expression, a mere residuum of Dionysian histrionism. For music to be made possible as a special art, quite a number of senses, and particularly the muscular sense, had to be paralysed (at least relatively: for all rhythm still appeals to our muscles to a certain extent): and thus man no longer imitates and represents physically everything he feels, as soon as he feels it. Nevertheless that is the normal Dionysian state, and in any case its primitive state. Music is the slowly attained specialisation of this state at the cost of kindred capacities.

11

The actor, the mime, the dancer, the musician, and the lyricist, are in their instincts fundamentally related; but they have gradually specialised in their particular branch, and become separated – even to the point of contradiction. The lyricist remained united with the musician for the longest period of time; and the actor with the dancer. The architect manifests neither a Dionysian nor an Apollonian state: In his case it is the great act of will, the will that moveth mountains, the ecstasy of the great will which aspires to art. The most powerful men have always inspired architects; the architect has always been under the suggestion of power. In the architectural structure, man's pride, man's triumph over gravitation, man's will to power, assume a visible form. Architecture is a sort of oratory of power by means of forms. Now it is persuasive, even flattering, and at other times merely commanding. The highest sensation of power and security finds expression in grandeur of style. That power which no longer requires to be proved, which scorns to please; which responds only with difficulty; which feels no witnesses around it; which is oblivious of the fact that it is being opposed; which relies on itself fatalistically, and is a law among laws: – such power expresses itself quite naturally in grandeur of style.

12

I have been reading the life of Thomas Carlyle, that unconscious and involuntary farce, that heroico-moral interpretation of dyspeptic moods. – Carlyle, a man of strong words and attitudes, a rhetorician by necessity, who seems ever to be tormented by the desire of finding some kind of strong faith, and by his inability to do so (– in this respect a typical Romanticist!). To yearn for a strong faith is not the proof of a strong faith, but rather the reverse. If a man have a strong faith he can indulge in the luxury of scepticism; he is strong enough, firm enough, well-knit enough for such a luxury. Carlyle stupefies something in himself by means of the *fortissimo* of his reverence for men of a strong faith, and his rage over those who are less foolish: he is in sore need of noise. An attitude of constant and passionate dishonesty towards himself – this is his *proprium*; by virtue of this he is and remains interesting. – Of course, in England he is admired precisely on account of his honesty. Well, that is English; and in view of the fact that the English are the nation of consummate cant, it is not only comprehensible but also very natural. At bottom, Carlyle is an English atheist who makes it a point of honour not to be one.

13

Emerson. – He is much more enlightened, much broader, more versatile, and more subtle than Carlyle; but above all, he is happier. He is one who instinctively lives on ambrosia and who leaves the indigestible parts of things on his plate. Compared with Carlyle he is a man of taste. – Carlyle, who was very fond of him, nevertheless declared that 'he does not give us enough to chew.' This is perfectly true but it is not unfavourable to Emerson. – Emerson possesses that kindly intellectual cheerfulness which deprecates overmuch seriousness; he has absolutely no idea of how old he is already, and how young he will yet be, – he could have said of himself, in Lope de Vega's words: '*yo me sucedo a mi mismo.*' His mind is always finding reasons for being contented and even thankful; and at times he gets preciously near to that serene superiority of the worthy bourgeois who returning from an amorous rendezvous *tamquam re bene gesta*, said gratefully '*Ut desint vires, tamen est laudanda voluptas.*'

14

Anti-Darwin. – As to the famous 'struggle for existence', it seems to me, for the present, to be more of an assumption than a fact. It does occur, but as an exception. The general condition of life is not one of want or famine, but rather of riches, of lavish luxuriance, and even of absurd prodigality, – where there is a struggle, it is a struggle for power. We should not confound Malthus with nature. – Supposing, however, that this struggle exists, – and it does indeed occur, – its result is unfortunately the very reverse of that which the Darwinian school seems to desire, and of that which in agreement with them we also might desire: that is to say, it is always to the disadvantage of the strong, the privileged, and the happy exceptions. Species do not evolve towards perfection: the weak always prevail over the strong – simply because they are the majority, and because they are also the more crafty. Darwin forgot the intellect (– that is English!), the

---

* An allusion to a verse in Luther's hymn: '*Lass fahren dahin... das Reich muss uns doch bleiben,*' which Nietzsche applies to the German Empire. – TR.

weak have more intellect. In order to acquire intellect, one must be in need of it. One loses it when one no longer needs it. He who possesses strength flings intellect to the deuce ('let it go hence!'** say the Germans of the present day, 'the *Empire* will remain'). As you perceive, intellect to me means caution, patience, craft, dissimulation, great self-control, and everything related to mimicry (what is praised nowadays as virtue is very closely related to the latter).

15

Casuistry of a Psychologist. – This man knows mankind: to what purpose does he study his fellows? He wants to derive some small or even great advantages from them, – he is a politician!... That man yonder is also well versed in human nature: and ye tell me that he wishes to draw no personal profit from his knowledge, that he is a thoroughly disinterested person? Examine him a little more closely! Maybe he wishes to derive a more wicked advantage from his possession; namely, to feel superior to men, to be able to look down upon them, no longer to feel one of them. This 'disinterested person' is a despiser of mankind; and the former is of a more humane type, whatever appearances may seem to say to the contrary. At least he considers himself the equal of those about him, at least he classifies himself with them.

16

The psychological tact of Germans seems to me to have been set in doubt by a whole series of cases which my modesty forbids me to enumerate. In one case at least I shall not let the occasion slip for substantiating my contention: I bear the Germans a grudge for having made a mistake about Kant and his 'backstairs philosophy', as I call it. Such a man was not the type of intellectual uprightness. Another thing I hate to hear is a certain infamous 'and': the Germans say, 'Goethe *and* Schiller', – I even fear that they say, 'Schiller and Goethe'.... Has nobody found Schiller out yet? – But there are other 'ands' which are even more egregious. With my own ears I have heard – only among University professors, it is true! – men speak of 'Schopenhauer *and* Hartmann'.**

** A disciple of Schopenhauer who blunted the sharpness of his master's Pessimism and who watered it down for modern requirements. – TR.

17

The most intellectual men, provided they are also the most courageous, experience the most excruciating tragedies: but on that very account they honour life, because it confronts them with its most formidable antagonism.

18

Concerning '*the Conscience of the Intellect*'. Nothing seems to me more uncommon today than genuine hypocrisy. I strongly suspect that this growth is unable to flourish in the mild climate of our culture. Hypocrisy belongs to an age of strong faith, – one in which one does not lose one's own faith in spite of the fact that one has to make an outward show of holding another faith. Nowadays a man gives it up; or, what is still more common, he acquires a second faith, – in any case, however, he remains honest. Without a doubt it is possible to have a much larger number of convictions at present, than it was formerly: *possible* – that is to say, allowable, – that is to say, *harmless*. From this there arises an attitude of toleration towards one's self. Toleration towards one's self allows of a greater number of convictions: the latter live comfortably side by side, and they take jolly good care, as all the world does today, not to compromise themselves. How does a man compromise himself today? When he is consistent; when he pursues a straight course; when he has anything less than five faces; when he is genuine.... I very greatly fear that modern man is much too fond of comfort for certain vices; and the consequence is that the latter are dying out. Everything evil which is the outcome of strength of will – and maybe there is nothing evil without the strengh of will, – degenerates, in our muggy atmosphere, into virtue. The few hypocrites I have known only imitated hypocrisy: like almost every tenth man today, they were actors. –

19

Beautiful and Ugly: – Nothing is more relative, let us say, more restricted, than our sense of the beautiful. He who would try to divorce it from the delight man finds in his fellows, would immediately lose his footing. 'Beauty in itself', is simply a word, it is not even a concept. In the beautiful, man postulates himself as the standard of perfection; in exceptional cases he worships himself as that standard.

A species has no other alternative than to say 'yea' to itself alone, in this way. Its lowest instinct, the instinct of self-preservation and self-expansion, still radiates in such sublimities. Man imagines the world itself to be overflowing with beauty, – he forgets that he is the cause of it all. He alone has endowed it with beauty. Alas! and only with human all-too-human beauty! Truth to tell man reflects himself in things, he thinks everything beautiful that throws his own image back at him. The judgment 'beautiful' is the 'vanity of his species'.... A little demon of suspicion may well whisper into the sceptic's ear: is the world really beautified simply because man thinks it beautiful? He has only humanised it – that is all. But nothing, absolutely nothing proves to us that it is precisely man who is the proper model of beauty. Who knows what sort of figure he would cut in the eyes of a higher judge of taste? He might seem a little *outré*? perhaps even somewhat amusing? perhaps a trifle arbitrary? 'O Dionysus, thou divine one, why dost thou pull mine ears?' Ariadne asks on one occasion of her philosophic lover, during one of those famous conversations on the island of Naxos. 'I find a sort of humour in thine ears, Ariadne: why are they not a little longer?'

20

Nothing is beautiful; man alone is beautiful: all æsthetic rests on this piece of ingenuousness, it is the first axiom of this science. And now let us straightway add the second to it: nothing is ugly save the degenerate man, – within these two first principles the realm of æsthetic judgments is confined. From the physiological standpoint, everything ugly weakens and depresses man. It reminds him of decay, danger, impotence; he literally loses strength in its presence. The effect of ugliness may be gauged by the dynamometer. Whenever man's spirits are downcast, it is a sign that he scents the proximity of something 'ugly'. His feeling of power, his will to power, his courage and his pride – these things collapse at the sight of what is ugly, and rise at the sight of what is beautiful. In both cases an inference is drawn; the premises to which are stored with extraordinary abundance in the instincts. Ugliness is understood to signify a hint and a symptom of degeneration: that which reminds us however remotely of degeneracy, impels us to the judgment 'ugly'. Every sign of exhaustion, of gravity, of age, of fatigue; every kind of constraint, such as cramp, or paralysis; and above all the smells, colours and forms associated with decomposition and putrefaction, however much they may have been attenuated into symbols, – all these things provoke the same reaction which is the judgment 'ugly'. A certain hatred expresses itself here: what is it that man hates? Without a doubt it is the *decline of his type*. In this regard his hatred springs from the deepest instincts of the race: there is horror, caution, profundity and far-reaching vision in this hatred, – it is the most profound hatred that exists. On its account alone Art is profound.

21

Schopenhauer. – Schopenhauer, the last German who is to be reckoned with (– who is a European event like Goethe, Hegel, or Heinrich Heine, and who is not merely local, national), is for a psychologist a case of the first rank: I mean as a malicious though masterly attempt to enlist on the side of a general nihilistic depreciation of life, the very forces which are opposed to such a movement, – that is to say, the great self-affirming powers of the 'will to live', the exuberant forms of life itself. He interpreted Art, heroism, genius, beauty, great sympathy, knowledge, the will to truth, and tragedy, one after the other, as the results of the denial, or of the need of the denial, of the 'will' – the greatest forgery, Christianity always excepted, which history has to show. Examined more carefully, he is in this respect simply the heir of the Christian interpretation; except that he knew how to approve in a Christian fashion (*i.e.*, nihilistically) even of the great facts of human culture, which Christianity completely repudiates. (He approved of them as paths to 'salvation', as preliminary stages to 'salvation', as *appetisers* calculated to arouse the desire for 'salvation'.)

22

Let me point to one single instance. Schopenhauer speaks of beauty with melancholy ardour, – why in sooth does he do this? Because in beauty he sees a bridge on which one can travel further, or which stimulates one's desire to travel further. According to him it constitutes a momentary emancipation from the 'will' – it lures to eternal salvation. He values it more particularly as a deliverance from the 'burning core of the will' which is sexuality, – in beauty he recognises the negation of the procreative instinct. Singular Saint! Someone contradicts thee;

I fear it is Nature. Why is there beauty of tone, colour, aroma, and of rhythmic movement in Nature at all? What is it forces beauty to the fore? Fortunately, too, a certain philosopher contradicts him. No less an authority than the divine Plato himself (thus does Schopenhauer call him), upholds another proposition: that all beauty lures to procreation, – that this precisely is the chief characteristic of its effect, from the lowest sensuality to the highest spirituality.

23

Plato goes further. With an innocence for which a man must be Greek and not 'Christian', he says that there would be no such thing as Platonic philosophy if there were not such beautiful boys in Athens: it was the sight of them alone that set the soul of the philosopher reeling with erotic passion, and allowed it no rest until it had planted the seeds of all lofty things in a soil so beautiful. He was also a singular saint! – One scarcely believes one's ears, even supposing one believes Plato. At least one realises that philosophy was pursued differently in Athens; above all, publicly. Nothing is less Greek than the cobweb-spinning with concepts by an anchorite, *amor intellectualis dei* after the fashion of Spinoza. Philosophy according to Plato's style might be defined rather as an erotic competition, as a continuation and a spiritualisation of the old agonal gymnastics and the conditions on which they depend.... What was the ultimate outcome of this philosophic eroticism of Plato's? A new art-form of the Greek *Agon*, dialectics. – In opposition to Schopenhauer and to the honour of Plato, I would remind you that all the higher culture and literature of classical France, as well, grew up on the soil of sexual interests. In all its manifestations you may look for gallantry, the senses, sexual competition, and 'woman', and you will not look in vain.

24

L'art pour l'art. – The struggle against a purpose in art is always a struggle against the moral tendency in art, against its subordination to morality. *L'art pour l'art means*, 'let morality go to the devil!' – But even this hostility betrays the preponderating power of the moral prejudice. If art is deprived of the purpose of preaching morality and of improving mankind, it does not by any means follow that art is absolutely pointless, purposeless, senseless, in short *l'art pour l'art*

– a snake which bites its own tail. 'No purpose at all is better than a moral purpose!' – thus does pure passion speak. A psychologist, on the other hand, puts the question: what does all art do? does it not praise? does it not glorify? does it not select? does it not bring things into prominence? In all this it strengthens or weakens certain valuations. Is this only a secondary matter? an accident? something in which the artist's instinct has no share? Or is it not rather the very prerequisite which enables the artist to accomplish something?... Is his most fundamental instinct concerned with art? Is it not rather concerned with the purpose of art, with life? with a certain desirable kind of life? Art is the great stimulus to life; how can it be regarded as purpose-less, as pointless, as *l'art pour l'art*? – There still remains one question to be answered: Art also reveals much that is ugly, hard and questionable in life, – does it not thus seem to make life intolerable? – And, as a matter of fact, there have been philosophers who have ascribed this function to art. According to Schopenhauer's doctrine, the general object of art was to 'free one from the Will'; and what he honoured as the great utility of tragedy, was that it 'made people more resigned'. – But this, as I have already shown, is a pessimistic standpoint; it is the 'evil eye': the artist himself must be appealed to. What is it that the soul of the tragic artist communicates to others? Is it not precisely his fearless attitude towards that which is terrible and questionable? This attitude is in itself a highly desirable one; he who has once, experienced it honours it above everything else. He communicates it. He must communicate, provided he is an artist and a genius in the art of communication. A courageous and free spirit, in the presence of a mighty foe, in the presence of a sublime misfortune, and face to face with a problem that inspires horror – this is the triumphant attitude which the tragic artist selects and which he glorifies. The martial elements in our soul celebrate their Saturnalia in tragedy; he who is used to suffering, he who looks out for suffering, the heroic man, extols his existence by means of tragedy, – to him alone does the tragic artist offer this cup of sweetest cruelty. –

25

To associate in an amiable fashion with anybody; to keep the house of one's heart open to all, is certainly liberal: but it is nothing else. One can recognise the hearts that are capable of noble hospitality, by their wealth of screened windows and closed shutters: they keep their best rooms empty. Whatever for? – Because they are expecting guests who are somebodies.

26

We no longer value ourselves sufficiently highly when we communicate our soul's content. Our real experiences are not at all garrulous. They could not communicate themselves even if they wished to. They are at a loss to find words for such confidences. Those things for which we find words, are things we have already overcome. In all speech there lies an element of contempt. Speech, it would seem, was only invented for average, mediocre and communicable things. – Every spoken word proclaims the speaker vulgarised – (Extract from a moral code for deaf-and-dumb people and other philosophers.)

27

'This picture is perfectly beautiful!'* The dissatisfied and exasperated literary woman with a desert in her heart and in her belly, listening with agonised curiosity every instant to the imperative which whispers to her from the very depths of her being: *aut liberi, aut libri*: the literary woman, sufficiently educated to understand the voice of nature, even when nature speaks Latin, and moreover enough of a peacock and a goose to speak even French with herself in secret '*Je me verrai, je me lirai, je m'extasierai et je dirai: Possible, que j'aie eu tant d'esprit?*' ...

28

The objective ones speak. – 'Nothing comes more easily to us, than to be wise, patient, superior. We are soaked in the oil of indulgence and of sympathy, we are absurdly just, we forgive everything. Precisely on that account we should be severe with ourselves; for that very reason we ought from time to time to go in for a little emotion, a little emotional vice. It may seem bitter to us; and between ourselves we may even laugh at the figure which it makes us cut. But what does it matter? We have no other kind of self-control left. This is our asceticism, our manner of performing penance.' *To become personal* – the virtues of the 'impersonal and objective one'.

---

* Quotation from the libretto of Mozart's 'Magic Flute' Act I, Sc. 3. – TR.

29

Extract from a doctor's examination paper. – 'What is the task of all higher schooling?' – To make man into a machine. 'What are the means employed?' – He must learn how to be bored. 'How is this achieved?' – By means of the concept of duty. 'What example of duty has he before his eyes?' – The philologist: it is he who teaches people how to swat. 'Who is the perfect man?' – The Government official. 'Which philosophy furnishes the highest formula for the Government official?' – Kant's philosophy: the Government official as thing-in-itself made judge over the Government official as appearance.

30

The right to stupidity. – The worn-out worker, whose breath is slow, whose look is good-natured, and who lets things slide just as they please: this typical figure which in this age of labour (and of 'Empire!') is to be met with in all classes of society, has now begun to appropriate even Art, including the book, above all the newspaper, – and how much more so beautiful nature, Italy! This man of the evening, with his 'savage instincts lulled', as Faust has it; needs his summer holiday, his sea-baths, his glacier, his Bayreuth. In such ages Art has the right to be *purely foolish*, – as a sort of vacation for spirit, wit and sentiment. Wagner understood this. Pure foolishness* is a pick-me-up....

31

Yet another problem of diet. – The means with which Julius Cæsar preserved himself against sickness and headaches: heavy marches, the simplest mode of living, uninterrupted sojourns in the open air, continual hardships, – generally speaking these are the self-preservative and self-defensive measures against the extreme vulnerability of those subtle machines working at the highest pressure, which are called geniuses.

32

The immoralist speaks. – Nothing is more distasteful to true philosophers than man when he begins to wish.... If they see man only at his deeds; if they see this bravest, craftiest and most enduring of animals even inextricably entangled in disaster, how admirable he then appears to

---

* This alludes to Parsifal. See my note on p. 96, vol. i., 'The Will to Power'. – TR.

them! They even encourage him.... But true philosophers despise the man who wishes, as also the 'desirable' man – and all the desiderata and *ideals* of man in general. If a philosopher could be a nihilist, he would be one; for he finds only nonentity behind all human ideals. Or, not even nonentity, but vileness, absurdity, sickness, cowardice, fatigue and all sorts of dregs from out the quaffed goblets of his life.... How is it that man, who as a reality is so estimable, ceases from deserving respect the moment he begins to desire? Must he pay for being so perfect as a reality? Must he make up for his deeds, for the tension of spirit and will which underlies all his deeds, by an eclipse of his powers in matters of the imagination and in absurdity? Hitherto the history of his desires has been the *partie honteuse* of mankind: one should take care not to read too deeply in this history. That which justifies man is his reality, – it will justify him to all eternity. How much more valuable is a real man than any other man who is merely the phantom of desires, of dreams of stinks and of lies? – than any kind of ideal man?... And the ideal man, alone, is what the philosopher cannot abide.

33

The natural value of egoism. – Selfishness has as much value as the physiological value of him who practises it: its worth may be great, or it may be worthless and contemptible. Every individual may be classified according to whether he represents the ascending or the descending line of life. When this is decided, a canon is obtained by means of which the value of his selfishness may be determined. If he represent the ascending line of life, his value is of course extraordinary – and for the sake of the collective life which in him makes one step *forward*, the concern about his maintenance, about procuring his optimum of conditions may even be extreme. The human unit, the 'individual', as the people and the philosopher have always understood him, is certainly an error: he is nothing in himself, no atom, no 'link in the chain', no mere heritage from the past, – he represents the whole direct line of mankind up to his own life.... If he represent declining development, decay, chronic degeneration, sickness (– illnesses are on the whole already the outcome of decline, and not the cause thereof), he is of little worth, and the purest equity would have him *take away* as little as possible from those who are lucky strokes of nature. He is then only a parasite upon them....

34

The Christian and the anarchist. – When the anarchist, as the mouthpiece of the decaying strata of society, raises his voice in splendid indignation for 'right', 'justice', 'equal rights', he is only groaning under the burden of his ignorance, which cannot understand *why* he actually suffers, – what his poverty consists of – the poverty of life. An instinct of causality is active in him: someone must be responsible for his being so ill at ease. His 'splendid indignation' alone relieves him somewhat, it is a pleasure for all poor devils to grumble – it gives them a little intoxicating sensation of power. The very act of complaining, the mere fact that one bewails one's lot, may lend such a charm to life that on that account alone, one is ready to endure it. There is a small dose of revenge in every lamentation. One casts one's afflictions, and, under certain circumstances, even one's baseness, in the teeth of those who are different, as if their condition were an injustice, an *iniquitous* privilege. 'Since I am a *blackguard* you ought to be one too.' It is upon such reasoning that revolutions are based. – To bewail one's lot is always despicable: it is always the outcome of weakness. Whether one ascribes one's afflictions to others or to *one's self*, it is all the same. The socialist does the former, the Christian, for instance, does the latter. That which is common to both attitudes, or rather that which is equally ignoble in them both, is the fact that somebody must be to *blame* if one suffers – in short that the sufferer drugs himself with the honey of revenge to allay his anguish. The objects towards which this lust of vengeance, like a lust of pleasure, are directed, are purely accidental causes. In all directions the sufferer finds reasons for cooling his petty passion for revenge. If he is a Christian, I repeat, he finds these reasons in himself. The Christian and the anarchist – both are decadents. But even when the Christian condemns, slanders, and sullies the world, he is actuated by precisely the same instinct as that which leads the socialistic workman to curse, calumniate and cast dirt at society. The last 'Judgment' itself is still the sweetest solace to revenge – revolution, as the socialistic workman expects it, only thought of as a little more remote.... The notion of a 'Beyond', as well – why a Beyond, if it be not a means of splashing mud over a 'Here', over this world?...

35

A criticism of the morality of decadence. – An 'altruistic' morality, a morality under which selfishness withers, is in all circumstances a bad sign. This is true of individuals and above all of nations. The best are lacking when selfishness begins to be lacking. Instinctively to select that which is harmful to one, to be *lured* by 'disinterested' motives, – these things almost provide the formula for decadence. 'Not to have one's own interests at heart' – this is simply a moral fig-leaf concealing a very different fact, a physiological one, to wit: – 'I no longer know how to find what is to my interest.'... Disintegration of the instincts! – All is up with man when he becomes altruistic. – Instead of saying ingenuously 'I am no longer any good,' the lie of morality in the decadent's mouth says: 'Nothing is any good, – life is no good.' – A judgment of this kind ultimately becomes a great danger; for it is infectious, and it soon flourishes on the polluted soil of society with tropical luxuriance, now as a religion (Christianity), anon as a philosophy (Schopenhauerism). In certain circumstances the mere effluvia of such a venomous vegetation, springing as it does out of the very heart of putrefaction, can poison life for thousands and thousands of years.

36

A moral for doctors. – The sick man is a parasite of society. In certain cases it is indecent to go on living. To continue to vegetate in a state of cowardly dependence upon doctors and special treatments, once the meaning of life, the right to life, has been lost, ought to be regarded with the greatest contempt by society. The doctors, for their part, should be the agents for imparting this contempt, – they should no longer prepare prescriptions, but should every day administer a fresh dose of *disgust* to their patients. A new responsibility should be created, that of the doctor – the responsibility of ruthlessly suppressing and eliminating *degenerate* life, in all cases in which the highest interests of life itself, of ascending life, demand such a course – for instance in favour of the right of procreation, in favour of the right of being born, in favour of the right to live. One should die proudly when it is no longer possible to live proudly. Death should be chosen freely, – death at the right time, faced clearly and joyfully and embraced while one is surrounded by one's children and other witnesses. It should be affected in such a way that a proper farewell is still possible, that he who is about to take leave of us is still *himself*, and really capable not only of valuing what he has achieved and willed in life, but also of *summing-up* the value of life itself. Everything precisely the opposite of the ghastly comedy which Christianity has made of the hour of death. We should never forgive Christianity for having so abused the weakness of the dying man as to do violence to his conscience, or for having used his manner of dying as a means of valuing both man and his past! – In spite of all cowardly prejudices, it is our duty, in this respect, above all to reinstate the proper – that is to say, the physiological, aspect of so-called *natural* death, which after all is perfectly 'unnatural' and nothing else than suicide. One never perishes through anybody's fault but one's own. The only thing is that the death which takes place in the most contemptible circumstances, the death that is not free, the death which occurs at the wrong time, is the death of a coward. Out of the very love one bears to life, one should wish death to be different from this – that is to say, free, deliberate, and neither a matter of chance nor of surprise. Finally let me whisper a word of advice to our friends the pessimists and all other decadents. We have not the power to prevent ourselves from being born: but this error – for sometimes it is an error – can be rectified if we choose. The man who does away with himself, performs the most estimable of deeds: he almost deserves to live for having done so. Society – nay, life itself, derives more profit from such a deed than from any sort of life spent in renunciation, anæmia and other virtues, – at least the suicide frees others from the sight of him, at least he removes one objection against life. Pessimism *pur et vert*, can *be proved only* by the self-refutation of the pessimists themselves: one should go a step further in one's consistency; one should not merely deny life with 'The World as Will and Idea', as Schopenhauer did; one should in the first place *deny Schopenhauer....* Incidentally, Pessimism, however infectious it may be, does not increase the morbidness of an age or of a whole species; it is rather the expression of that morbidness. One falls a victim to it in the same way as one falls a victim to cholera; one must already be predisposed to the disease. Pessimism in itself does not increase the number of the world's *decadents* by a single unit. Let me remind you of the statistical fact that in those years in which cholera rages, the total number of deaths does not exceed that of other years.

37

Have we become more moral? – As might have been expected, the whole *ferocity* of moral stultification, which, as is well known, passes for morality itself in Germany, hurled itself against my concept 'Beyond Good and Evil'. I could tell you some nice tales about this. Above all, people tried to make me see the 'incontestable superiority' of our age in regard to moral sentiment, and the progress we had made in these matters. Compared with us, a Cæsar Borgia was by no means to be represented as 'higher man', the sort of *Superman*, which I declared him to be. The editor of the Swiss paper the *Bund* went so far as not only to express his admiration for the courage displayed by my enterprise, but also to pretend to 'understand' that the intended purpose of my work was to abolish all decent feeling. Much obliged! – In reply, I venture to raise the following question: *have we really become more moral?* The fact that everybody believes that we have is already an objection to the belief. We modern men, so extremely delicate and susceptible, full of consideration one for the other, actually dare to suppose that the pampering fellow-feeling which we all display, this unanimity which we have at last acquired in sparing and helping and trusting one another marks a definite step forward, and shows us to be far ahead of the man of the Renaissance. But every age thinks the same, it is *bound* to think the same. This at least, is certain, that we should not dare to stand amid the conditions which prevailed at the Renaissance, we should not even dare to imagine ourselves in those conditions: our nerves could not endure that reality, not to speak of our muscles. The inability to do this however does not denote any progress; but simply the different and more senile quality of our particular nature, its greater weakness, delicateness, and susceptibility, out of which a morality *more rich in consideration* was bound to arise. If we imagine our delicateness and senility, our physiological decrepitude as non-existent, our morality of 'humanisation' would immediately lose all value – no morality has any value *per se* – it would even fill us with scorn. On the other hand, do not let us doubt that we moderns, wrapped as we are in the thick cotton wool of our humanitarianism which would shrink even from grazing a stone, would present a comedy to Cæsar Borgia's contemporaries which would literally make them die of laughter. We are indeed, without knowing it, exceedingly ridiculous with our modern 'virtues'…. The decline of the instincts of hostility and of those instincts that arouse suspicion, – for this if anything is what constitutes our progress – is only one of the results manifested by the general decline in *vitality*: it requires a hundred times more trouble and caution to live such a dependent and senile existence. In such circumstances everybody gives everybody else a helping hand, and, to a certain extent, everybody is either an invalid or an invalid's attendant. This is then called 'virtue': among those men who knew a different life – that is to say, a fuller, more prodigal, more superabundant sort of life, it might have been called by another name, – possibly 'cowardice', or 'vileness', or 'old woman's morality'.... Our mollification of morals – this is my cry; this if you will is my *innovation* – is the outcome of our decline; conversely hardness and terribleness in morals may be the result of a surplus of life. When the latter state prevails, much is dared, much is challenged, and much is also *squandered*. That which formerly was simply the salt of life, would now be our *poison*. To be indifferent – even this is a form of strength – for that, likewise, we are too senile, too decrepit: our morality of fellow-feeling, against which I was the first to raise a finger of warning, that which might be called *moral impressionism*, is one symptom the more of the excessive physiological irritability which is peculiar to everything decadent. That movement which attempted to introduce itself in a scientific manner on the shoulders of Schopenhauer's morality of pity – a very sad attempt! – is in its essence the movement of decadence in morality, and as such it is intimately related to Christian morality. Strong ages and noble cultures see something contemptible in pity, in the 'love of one's neighbour', and in a lack of egoism and of self-esteem. – Ages should be measured according to their *positive forces*; – valued by this standard that prodigal and fateful age of the Renaissance, appears as the last *great age*, while we moderns with our anxious care of ourselves and love of our neighbours, with all our unassuming virtues of industry, equity, and scientific method – with our lust of collection, of economy and of mechanism – represent a *weak* age.... Our virtues are necessarily determined, and are even stimulated, by our weakness. 'Equality', a certain definite process of making everybody uniform, which only finds its expression in the theory of equal rights, is essentially bound up with a declining culture: the chasm between man and man, class and class, the multiplicity of types, the will to be one's self, and to distinguish one's self – that, in fact, which I call the *pathos of distance* is proper to all *strong* ages. The force of tension, – nay, the tension itself, between extremes grows slighter every day, – the extremes themselves are tending to become obliterated to the point of becoming identical. All our political theories and state constitutions, not by any means excepting 'The German Empire', are the logical consequences, the necessary consequences of decline; the unconscious effect of *decadence* has begun to dominate even the ideals of the various sciences. My objection to the whole of English and French sociology still continues to be this, that it knows only the *decadent form* of society from experience, and with perfectly childlike innocence takes the instincts of decline as the *norm*, the standard, of sociological valuations. *Descending* life, the decay of all organising power – that is to say, of all that power which separates, cleaves gulfs, and establishes rank above and below, formulated itself in modern sociology as the ideal. Our socialists are decadents: but Herbert Spencer was also a *decadent*, – he saw something to be desired in the triumph of altruism!…

38

My concept of freedom. – Sometimes the value of a thing does not lie in that which it helps us to achieve, but in the amount we have to pay for it, – what it costs us. For instance, liberal institutions straightway cease from being liberal, the moment they are soundly established: once this is attained no more grievous and more thorough enemies of freedom exist than liberal institutions! One knows, of course, what they bring about: they undermine the Will to Power, they are the levelling of mountain and valley exalted to a morality, they make people small, cowardly and pleasure-loving, – by means of them the gregarious animal invariably triumphs. Liberalism, or, in plain English, the *transformation of mankind into cattle*. The same institutions, so long as they are fought for, produce quite other results; then indeed they promote the cause of freedom quite powerfully. Regarded more closely, it is war which produces these results, war in favour of liberal institutions, which, as war, allows the illiberal instincts to subsist. For war trains men to be free. What in sooth is freedom? Freedom is the will to be responsible for ourselves. It is to preserve the distance which separates us from other men. To grow more indifferent to hardship, to severity, to privation, and even to life itself. To be ready to sacrifice men for one's cause, one's self included. Freedom denotes that the virile instincts which rejoice in war and in victory, prevail over other instincts; for instance, over the instincts of 'happiness'. The man who has won his freedom, and how much more so, therefore, the spirit that has won its freedom, tramples ruthlessly upon that contemptible kind of comfort which tea-grocers, Christians, cows, women, Englishmen and other democrats worship in their dreams. The free man is a *warrior*. – How is freedom measured in individuals as well as in nations? According to the resistance which has to be overcome, according to the pains which it costs to remain *uppermost*. The highest type of free man would have to be sought where the greatest resistance has continually to be overcome: five paces away from tyranny, on the very threshold of the danger of thraldom. This is psychologically true if, by the word 'tyrants' we mean inexorable and terrible instincts which challenge the *maximum* amount of authority and discipline to oppose them – the finest example of this is Julius Cæsar; it is also true politically: just examine the course of history. The nations which were worth anything, which got to be worth anything, never attained to that condition under liberal institutions: *great danger* made out of them something which deserves reverence, that danger which alone can make us aware of our resources, our virtues, our means of defence, our weapons, our *genius* – which *compels* us to be strong. *First* principle: a man must need to be strong, otherwise he will never attain it. – Those great forcing-houses of the strong, of the strongest kind of men that have ever existed on earth, the aristocratic communities like those of Rome and Venice, understood freedom precisely as I understand the word: as something that one has and that one has not, as something that one *will* have and that one *seizes by force*.

39

A criticism of modernity. – Our institutions are no longer any good; on this point we are all agreed. But the fault does not lie with them; but with *us*. Now that we have lost all the instincts out of which institutions grow, the latter on their part are beginning to disappear from our midst because we are no longer fit for them. Democracy has always been the death agony of the power of organisation: already in 'Human All-too-Human', Part I., Aph. 472, I pointed out that modern democracy, together with its half-measures, of which the 'German

Empire' is an example, was a decaying form of the State. For institutions to be possible there must exist a sort of will, instinct, imperative, which cannot be otherwise than antiliberal to the point of wickedness: the will to tradition, to authority, to responsibility for centuries to come, to *solidarity* in long family lines forwards and backwards *in infinitum*. If this will is present, something is founded which resembles the *imperium Romanum*; or Russia, the *only* great nation today that has some lasting power and grit in her, that can bide her time, that can still promise something. – Russia the opposite of all wretched European petty-statism and neurasthenia, which the foundation of the German Empire has brought to a crisis. The whole of the Occident no longer possesses those instincts from which institutions spring, out of which a *future* grows: maybe nothing is more opposed to its 'modern spirit' than these things. People live for the present, they live at top speed – they certainly live without any sense of responsibility; and this is precisely what they call 'freedom'. Everything in institutions which makes them institutions, is scorned, loathed and repudiated: everybody is in mortal fear of a new slavery, wherever the word 'authority' is so much as whispered. The decadence of the valuing instinct, both in our politicians and in our political parties, goes so far, that they instinctively prefer that which acts as a solvent, that which precipitates the final catastrophe…. As an example of this behold *modern* marriage. All reason has obviously been divorced from modern marriage: but this is no objection to matrimony itself but to modernity. The rational basis of marriage – it lay in the exclusive legal responsibility of the man: by this means some ballast was laid in the ship of matrimony, whereas nowadays it has a list, now on this side, now on that. The rational basis of marriage – it lay in its absolute indissolubleness: in this way it was given a gravity which knew how to make its influence felt, in the face of the accident of sentiment, passion and momentary impulse: it lay also in the fact that the responsibility of choosing the parties to the contract, lay with the families. By showing ever more and more favour to *love*-marriages, the very foundation of matrimony, that which alone makes it an institution, has been undermined. No institution ever has been nor ever will be built upon an idiosyncrasy; as I say, marriage cannot be based upon 'love'. It can be based upon sexual desire; upon the instinct of property (wife and child as possessions); upon the instinct of dominion, which constantly organises for itself the smallest form of dominion, – the family which *requires* children and heirs in order to hold fast, also in the physiological sense, to a certain quantum of acquired power, influence and wealth, so as to prepare for lasting tasks, and for solidarity in the instincts from one century to another. Marriage as an institution presupposes the affirmation of the greatest and most permanent form of organisation; if society cannot as a whole *stand security* for itself into the remotest generations, marriage has no meaning whatsoever. – Modern marriage *has lost* its meaning; consequently it is being abolished.

40

The question of the working-man. – The mere fact that there is such a thing as the question of the working-man is due to stupidity, or at bottom to degenerate instincts which are the cause of all the stupidity of modern times. Concerning certain things *no questions ought to be put*: the first imperative principle of instinct. For the life of me I cannot see what people want to do with the working-man of Europe, now that they have made a question of him. He is far too comfortable to cease from questioning ever more and more, and with ever less modesty. After all, he has the majority on his side. There is now not the slightest hope that an unassuming and contented sort of man, after the style of the Chinese, will come into being in this quarter: and this would have been the reasonable course, it was even a dire necessity. What has been done? Everything has been done with the view of nipping the very prerequisite of this accomplishment in the bud with the most frivolous thoughtlessness those self-same instincts by means of which a working-class becomes possible, and tolerable even to its members themselves, have been destroyed root and branch. The working-man has been declared fit for military service; he has been granted the right of combination, and of voting: can it be wondered at that he already regards his condition as one of distress (expressed morally, as an injustice)? But, again I ask, what do people want? If they desire a certain end, then they should desire the means thereto. If they will have slaves, then it is madness to educate them to be masters.

41

'The kind of freedom I do *not* mean....'* – In an age like the present, it simply adds to one's perils to be left to one's instincts. The instincts contradict, disturb, and destroy each other; I have already defined modernism as physiological self-contradiction. A reasonable system of education would insist upon at least one of these instinct-systems being *paralysed* beneath an iron pressure, in order to allow others to assert their power, to grow strong, and to dominate. At present, the only conceivable way of making the individual possible would be to *prune* him: – of making him possible – that is to say, *whole*. The very reverse occurs. Independence, free development, and *laisser aller* are clamoured for most violently precisely by those for whom no restraint *could be too sever*e – this is true *in politics*, it is true in Art. But this is a symptom of decadence: our modern notion of 'freedom' is one proof the more of the degeneration of instinct.

42

Where faith is necessary. – Nothing is more rare among moralists and saints than uprightness; maybe they say the reverse is true, maybe they even believe it. For, when faith is more useful, more effective, more convincing than *conscious* hypocrisy, by instinct that hypocrisy forthwith becomes *innocent*: first principle towards the understanding of great saints. The same holds good of philosophers, that other order of saints; their whole business compels them to concede only certain truths – that is to say, those by means of which their particular trade receives the *public* sanction, – to speak 'Kantingly': the truths of *practical* reason. They know what they *must* prove; in this respect they are practical, – they recognise each other by the fact that they agree upon 'certain truths'. – 'Thou shalt not lie' – in plain English: – *Beware*, Mr Philosopher, of speaking the truth....

43

A quiet hint to conservatives. – That which we did not know formerly, and know now, or might know if we chose, – is the fact that a *retrograde formation*, a reversion in any sense or degree, is absolutely impossible. We physiologists, at least, are aware of this. But all priests and moralists have believed in it, – they wished to drag and screw man back to a

---

*   This is a playful adaptation of Max von Schenkendorf's poem 'Freiheit' The proper line reads: 'Freiheit die ich meine' (The freedom that I do mean). – TR.

former standard of virtue. Morality has always been a Procrustean bed. Even the politicians have imitated the preachers of virtue in this matter. There are parties at the present day whose one aim and dream is to make all things adopt the *crab-march*. But not everyone can be a crab. It cannot be helped: we must go forward, – that is to say step by step further and further into decadence (– this is my definition of modern 'progress'). We can hinder this development, and by so doing dam up and accumulate degeneration itself and render it more convulsive, more *volcanic*: we cannot do more.

44

My concept of genius. – Great men, like great ages, are explosive material, in which a stupendous amount of power is accumulated; the first conditions of their existence are always historical and physiological; they are the outcome of the fact that for long ages energy has been collected, hoarded up, saved up and preserved for their use, and that no explosion has taken place. When the tension in the bulk has become sufficiently excessive, the most fortuitous stimulus suffices in order to call 'genius', 'great deeds', and momentous fate into the world. What then is the good of all environment, historical periods, '*Zeitgeist*' (Spirit of the age) and 'public opinion'? – Take the case of Napoleon. France of the Revolution, and still more of the period preceding the Revolution, would have brought forward a type which was the very reverse of Napoleon: it actually *did* produce such a type. And because Napoleon was something different, the heir of a stronger, more lasting and older civilisation than that which in France was being smashed to atoms he became master there, he was the only master there. Great men are necessary, the age in which they appear is a matter of chance; the fact that they almost invariably master their age is accounted for simply by the fact that they are stronger, that they are older, and that power has been stored longer for them. The relation of a genius to his age is that which exists between strength and weakness and between maturity and youth: the age is relatively always very much younger, thinner, less mature, less resolute and more childish. The fact that the general opinion in France at the present day, is utterly different on this very point (in Germany too, but that is of no consequence); the fact that in that country the theory of environment – a regular neuropathic notion – has become sacrosanct and almost scientific, and finds acceptance even among the physiologists, is a very bad, and exceedingly depressing sign. In England too the same belief prevails: but nobody will be surprised at that. The Englishman knows only two ways of understanding the genius and the 'great man': either *democratically* in the style of Buckle, or *religiously* after the manner of Carlyle. – The danger which great men and great ages represent, is simply extraordinary; every kind of exhaustion and of sterility follows in their wake. The great man is an end; the great age – the Renaissance for instance, – is an end. The genius – in work and in deed, – is necessarily a squanderer: the fact that he spends himself constitutes his greatness. The instinct of self-preservation is as it were suspended in him; the overpowering pressure of out-flowing energy in him forbids any such protection and prudence. People call this 'self-sacrifice', they praise his 'heroism', his indifference to his own well-being, his utter devotion to an idea, a great cause, a fatherland: All misunderstandings…. He flows out, he flows over, he consumes himself, he does not spare himself – and does all this with fateful necessity, irrevocably, involuntarily, just as a river involuntarily bursts its dams. But, owing to the fact that humanity has been much indebted to such explosives, it has endowed them with many things, for instance, with a kind of *higher morality*…. This is indeed the sort of gratitude that humanity is capable of: it *misunderstands* its benefactors.

45

The criminal and his like. – The criminal type is the type of the strong man amid unfavourable conditions, a strong man made sick. He lacks the wild and savage state, a form of nature and existence which is freer and more dangerous, in which everything that constitutes the shield and the sword in the instinct of the strong man, takes a place by right. Society puts a ban upon his virtues; the most spirited instincts inherent in him immediately become involved with the depressing passions, with suspicion, fear and dishonour. But this is almost the recipe for physiological degeneration. When a man has to do that which he is best suited to do, which he is most fond of doing, not only clandestinely, but also with long suspense, caution and ruse, he becomes anæmic; and inasmuch as he is always having to pay for his instincts in the form of danger, persecution and fatalities, even his feelings begin to turn against these instincts – he begins to regard them as fatal. It is society, our tame, mediocre, castrated society, in which an untutored son of nature who comes to us from his mountains or from his adventures at sea, must necessarily degenerate into a criminal. Or almost necessarily: for there are cases in which such a man shows himself to be stronger than society: the Corsican Napoleon is the most celebrated case of this. Concerning the problem before us, Dostoevsky's testimony is of importance – Dostoevsky who, incidentally, was the only psychologist from whom I had anything to learn: he belongs to the happiest windfalls of my life, happier even than the discovery of Stendhal. This profound man, who was right ten times over in esteeming the superficial Germans low, found the Siberian convicts among whom he lived for many years, – those thoroughly hopeless criminals for whom no road back to society stood open – very different from what even he had expected, – that is to say carved from about the best, hardest and most valuable material that grows on Russian soil.* Let us generalise the case of the criminal; let us imagine creatures who for some reason or other fail to meet with public approval, who know that they are regarded neither as beneficent nor useful, – the feeling of the Chandala, who are aware that they are not looked upon as equal, but as proscribed, unworthy, polluted. The thoughts and actions of all such natures are tainted with a subterranean mouldiness; everything in them is of a paler hue than in those on whose existence the sun shines. But almost all those creatures whom, nowadays, we honour and respect, formerly lived in this semi-sepulchral atmosphere: the man of science, the artist, the genius, the free spirit, the actor, the business man, and the great explorer. As long as the *priest* represented the highest type of man, every valuable kind of man was depreciated.... The time is coming – this I guarantee – when he will pass as the *lowest* type, as our Chandala, as the falsest and most disreputable kind of man.... I call your attention to the fact that even now, under the sway of the mildest customs and usages which have ever ruled on earth or at least in Europe, every form of standing aside, every kind of prolonged, excessively prolonged concealment, every unaccustomed and obscure form of existence tends to approximate to that type which the criminal exemplifies to perfection. All pioneers of the spirit have, for a while, the grey and fatalistic mark of the Chandala on their brows: *not* because

---

* See 'Memoirs of a House of the Dead', by Dostoevsky (translation by Marie von Thilo: 'Buried Alive'). – TR.

they are regarded as Chandala, but because they themselves feel the terrible chasm which separates them from all that is traditional and honourable. Almost every genius knows the 'Catilinarian life' as one of the stages in his development, a feeling of hate, revenge and revolt against everything that exists, that has ceased to evolve.... Catiline – the early stage of every Cæsar.

46

Here the outlook is free. – When a philosopher holds his tongue it may be the sign of the loftiness of his soul: when he contradicts himself it may be love; and the very courtesy of a knight of knowledge may force him to lie. It has been said, and not without subtlety: – *il est indigne des grands cœurs de répandre le trouble qu'ils ressentent*:** but it is necessary to add that there may also be *grandeur de cœur* in not shrinking *from the most undignified proceeding*. A woman who loves sacrifices her honour; a knight of knowledge who 'loves', sacrifices perhaps his humanity; a God who loved, became a Jew....

47

Beauty no accident. – Even the beauty of a race or of a family, the charm and perfection of all its movements, is attained with pains: like genius it is the final result of the accumulated work of generations. Great sacrifices must have been made on the altar of good taste, for its sake many things must have been done, and much must have been left undone – the seventeenth century in France is admirable for both of these things, – in this century there must have been a principle of selection in respect to company, locality, clothing, the gratification of the instinct of sex; beauty must have been preferred to profit, to habit, to opinion and to indolence. The first rule of all: – nobody must 'let himself go', not even when he is alone. – Good things are exceedingly costly: and in all cases the law obtains that he who possesses them is a different person from him who is *acquiring* them. Everything good is an inheritance: that which is not inherited is imperfect, it is simply a beginning. In Athens at the time of Cicero – who expresses his surprise at the fact – the men and youths were by far superior in

---

** Clothilde de Veaux. – TR.

beauty to the women: but what hard work and exertions the male sex had for centuries imposed upon itself in the service of beauty! We must not be mistaken in regard to the method employed here: the mere discipline of feelings and thoughts is little better than nil (– it is in this that the great error of German culture, which is quite illusory, lies): the *body* must be persuaded first. The strict maintenance of a distinguished and tasteful demeanour, the obligation of frequenting only those who do not 'let themselves go', is amply sufficient to render one distinguished and tasteful: in two or three generations everything has already *taken deep root*. The fate of a people and of humanity is decided according to whether they begin culture at the right place – not at the 'soul' (as the fatal superstition of the priests and half-priests would have it): the *right place* is the body, demeanour, diet, physiology – the rest follows as the night the day.... That is why the Greeks remain the *first event in culture* – they knew and they *did* what was needful. Christianity with its contempt of the body is the greatest mishap that has ever befallen mankind.

48

Progress in my sense. – I also speak of a 'return to nature', although it is not a process of going back but of going up – up into lofty, free and even terrible nature and naturalness; such a nature as can play with great tasks and *may* play with them.... To speak in a *parable*. Napoleon was an example of a 'return to nature', as I understand it (for instance *in rebus tacticis*, and still more, as military experts know, in strategy). But Rousseau – whither did he want to return? Rousseau this first modern man, idealist and *canaille* in one person; who was in need of moral 'dignity', in order even to endure the sight of his own person, – ill with unbridled vanity and wanton self-contempt; this abortion, who planted his tent on the threshold of modernity, also wanted a 'return to nature'; but, I ask once more, whither did he wish to return? I hate Rousseau, even in the Revolution itself: the latter was the historical expression of this hybrid of idealist and *canaille*. The bloody farce which this Revolution ultimately became, its 'immorality', concerns me but slightly; what I loathe however is its Rousseauesque *morality* – the so-called 'truths' of the Revolution, by means of which it still exercises power and draws all flat and mediocre things over to its side. The doctrine of equality!... But there is no more deadly poison than this; for it *seems* to proceed from the very lips of justice, whereas in reality it draws the curtain down on all justice.... 'To equals equality, to unequals inequality' – that would be the real speech of justice and that which follows from it 'Never make unequal things equal.' The fact that so much horror and blood are associated with this doctrine of equality, has lent this 'modern idea' *par excellence* such a halo of fire and glory, that the Revolution as a drama has misled even the most noble minds. – That after all is no reason for honouring it the more. – I can see only one who regarded it as it should be regarded – that is to say, with *loathing*; I speak of Goethe.

49

Goethe. – No mere German, but a European event: a magnificent attempt to overcome the eighteenth century by means of a return to nature, by means of an ascent to the naturalness of the Renaissance, a kind of self-overcoming on the part of the century in question. – He bore the strongest instincåts of this century in his breast: its sentimentality, and idolatry of nature, its anti-historic, idealistic, unreal, and revolutionary spirit (– the latter is only a form of the unreal). He enlisted history, natural science, antiquity, as well as Spinoza, and above all practical activity, in his service. He drew a host of very definite horizons around him; far from liberating himself from life, he plunged right into it; he did not give in; he took as much as he could on his own shoulders, and into his heart. That to which he aspired was *totality*; he was opposed to the sundering of reason, sensuality, feeling and will (as preached with most repulsive scholasticism by Kant, the antipodes of Goethe); he disciplined himself into a harmonious whole, he *created* himself. Goethe in the midst of an age of unreal sentiment, was a convinced realist: he said yea to everything that was like him in this regard – there was no greater event in his life than that *ens realissimum*, surnamed Napoleon. Goethe conceived a strong, highly-cultured man, skilful in all bodily accomplishments, able to keep himself in check, having a feeling of reverence for himself, and so constituted as to be able to risk the full enjoyment of naturalness in all its rich profusion and be strong enough for this freedom; a man of tolerance, not out of weakness but out of strength, because he knows how to turn to his own profit that which would ruin the mediocre nature; a man unto whom nothing is any longer forbidden, unless it be weakness either as a vice or as a virtue. Such a spirit, *become free*, appears in the middle of the universe with a feeling of cheerful and confident fatalism; he believes that only individual things are bad, and that as a whole the universe justifies and, affirms itself – *He no longer denies....* But such a faith is the highest of all faiths: I christened it with the name of Dionysus.

50

It might be said that, in a certain sense, the nineteenth century also strove after all that Goethe himself aspired to: catholicity in understanding, in approving; a certain reserve towards everything, daring realism, and a reverence for every fact. How is it that the total result of this is not a Goethe, but a state of chaos, a nihilistic groan, an inability to discover where one is, an instinct of fatigue which *in praxi* is persistently driving Europe *to hark back to the eighteenth century*? (– For instance in the form of maudlin romanticism, altruism, hyper-sentimentality, pessimism in taste, and socialism in politics). Is not the nineteenth century, at least in its closing years, merely an accentuated, brutalised eighteenth century, – that is to say a century of decadence? And has not Goethe been – not alone for Germany, but also for the whole of Europe, – merely an episode, a beautiful 'in vain'? But great men are misunderstood when they are regarded from the wretched standpoint of public utility. The fact that no advantage can be derived from them – *this in itself may perhaps be peculiar to greatness.*

51

Goethe is the last German whom I respect: he had understood three things as I understand them. We also agree as to the 'cross'.* People often ask me why on earth I write in *German*: nowhere am I less read than in the Fatherland. But who knows whether I even *desire* to be read at present? – To create things on which time may try its teeth in vain; to be concerned both in the form and the substance of my writing, about a certain degree of immortality – never have I been modest enough to demand less of myself. The aphorism, the sentence, in both of which I, as the first among Germans, am a master, are the forms of 'eternity'; it is my ambition to say in ten sentences what

---

* See my note on p. 147 of Vol. I. of the *Will to Power*. – TR.

everyone else says in a whole book, – what everyone else does *not* say in a whole book.

I have given mankind the deepest book it possesses, my *Zarathustra*; before long I shall give it the most independent one.

THINGS I OWE TO THE ANCIENTS

1

In conclusion I will just say a word concerning that world to which I have sought new means of access, to which I may perhaps have found a new passage – the ancient world. My taste, which is perhaps the reverse of tolerant, is very far from saying yea through and through even to this world: on the whole it is not over eager to say *yea*, it would prefer to say *nay*, and better still nothing whatever.... This is true of whole cultures; it is true of books, – it is also true of places and of landscapes. Truth to tell, the number of ancient books that count for something in my life is but small; and the most famous are not of that number. My sense of style, for the epigram as style, was awakened almost spontaneously upon my acquaintance with Sallust. I have not forgotten the astonishment of my respected teacher Corssen, when he was forced to give his worst Latin pupil the highest marks, – at one stroke I had learned all there was to learn. Condensed, severe, with as much substance as possible in the background, and with cold but roguish hostility towards all 'beautiful words' and 'beautiful feelings' – in these things I found my own particular bent. In my writings up to my 'Zarathustra', there will be found a very earnest ambition to attain to the *Roman* style, to the '*ære perennius*' in style. – The same thing happened on my first acquaintance with Horace. Up to the present no poet has given me the same artistic raptures as those which from the first I received from an Horatian ode. In certain languages it would be absurd even to aspire to what is accomplished by this poet. This mosaic of words, in which every unit spreads its power to the left and to the right over the whole, by its sound, by its place in the sentence, and by its meaning, this *minimum* in the compass and number of the signs, and the *maximum* of energy in the signs which is thereby achieved – all this is Roman, and, if you will believe me, noble *par excellence*. By the side of this all the rest of poetry becomes something popular, – nothing more than senseless sentimental twaddle.

2

I am not indebted to the Greeks for anything like such strong impressions; and, to speak frankly, they cannot be to us what the Romans are. One cannot *learn* from the Greeks – their style is too strange, it is also too fluid, to be imperative or to have the effect of a classic. Who would ever have learnt writing from a Greek! Who would ever have learned it without the Romans!... Do not let anyone suggest Plato to me. In regard to Plato I am a thorough sceptic, and have never been able to agree to the admiration of Plato the *artist*, which is traditional among scholars. And after all, in this matter, the most refined judges of taste in antiquity are on my side. In my opinion Plato bundles all the forms of style pell-mell together, in this respect he is one of the first decadents of style: he has something similar on his conscience to that which the Cynics had who invented the *satura Menippea*. For the Platonic dialogue – this revoltingly self-complacent and childish kind of dialectics – to exercise any charm over you, you must never have read any good French authors, – Fontenelle for instance. Plato is boring. In reality my distrust of Plato is fundamental. I find him so very much astray from all the deepest instincts of the Hellenes, so steeped in moral prejudices, so pre-existently Christian – the concept 'good' is already the highest value with him, – that rather than use any other expression I would prefer to designate the whole phenomenon Plato with the hard word 'superior bunkum', or, if you would like it better, 'idealism'. Humanity has had to pay dearly for this Athenian having gone to school among the Egyptians (– or among the Jews in Egypt?...). In the great fatality of Christianity, Plato is that double-faced fascination called the 'ideal', which made it possible for the more noble natures of antiquity to misunderstand themselves and to tread the *bridge* which led to the 'cross'. And what an amount of Plato is still to be found in the concept 'church', and in the construction, the system and the practice of the church! – My recreation, my predilection, my cure, after all Platonism, has always been Thucydides. Thucydides and perhaps Machiavelli's *principe* are most closely related to me owing to the absolute determination which they show of refusing to deceive themselves and of seeing reason in *reality*, – not in 'rationality', and still less in 'morality'. There is no more radical cure than Thucydides for the lamentably rose-coloured idealisation of the Greeks which the 'classically-cultured' stripling bears with him into life, as a reward for his public school training. His writings must be carefully studied line by line, and his unuttered thoughts must be read as distinctly as what he actually says. There are few thinkers so rich in unuttered thoughts. In him the culture 'of the Sophists' – that is to say, the culture of realism, receives its most perfect expression: this inestimable movement in the midst of the moral and idealistic knavery of the Socratic Schools which was then breaking out in all directions. Greek philosophy is the decadence of the Greek instinct: Thucydides is the great summing up, the final manifestation of that strong, severe positivism which lay in the instincts of the ancient Hellene. After all, it is courage in the face of reality that distinguishes such natures as Thucydides from Plato: Plato is a coward in the face of reality – consequently he takes refuge in the ideal: Thucydides is master of himself, – consequently he is able to master life.

3

To rout up cases of 'beautiful souls', 'golden means' and other perfections among the Greeks, to admire, say, their calm grandeur, their ideal attitude of mind, their exalted simplicity – from this 'exalted simplicity', which after all is a piece of *niaiserie allemande*, I was preserved by the psychologist within me. I saw their strongest instinct, the Will to Power, I saw them quivering with the fierce violence of this instinct, – I saw all their institutions grow out of measures of security calculated to preserve each member of their society from the inner *explosive material* that lay in his neighbour's breast. This enormous internal tension thus discharged itself in terrible and reckless hostility outside the state: the various states mutually tore each other to bits, in order that each individual state could remain at peace with itself. It was then necessary to be strong; for danger lay close at hand, – it lurked in ambush everywhere. The superb suppleness of their bodies, the daring realism and immorality which is peculiar to the Hellenes, was a necessity not an inherent quality. It was a result, it had not been there from the beginning. Even their festivals and their arts were but means in producing a feeling of superiority, and of showing it: they are measures of self-glorification; and in certain circumstances of making one's self terrible.... Fancy judging the Greeks in the German style, from their philosophers; fancy using the suburban respectability of the Socratic schools as a key to what is fundamentally Hellenic!... The philosophers are of course the decadents of Hellas, the counter-movement directed against the old and noble taste (– against the agonal instinct, against the *polis*, against the value of the race, against the authority of tradition). Socratic virtues were preached to the Greeks, *because* the Greeks had lost virtue: irritable, cowardly, unsteady, and all turned to play-actors, they had more than sufficient reason to submit to having morality preached to them. Not that it helped them in any way; but great words and attitudes are so becoming to decadents.

4

I was the first who, in order to understand the ancient, still rich and even superabundant Hellenic instinct, took that marvellous phenomenon, which bears the name of Dionysus, seriously: it can be explained only as a manifestation of excessive energy. Whoever had studied the Greeks, as that most profound of modern connoisseurs of their culture, Jakob Burckhardt of Basle, had done, knew at once that something had been achieved by means of this interpretation. And in his '*Cultur der Griechen*' Burckhardt inserted a special chapter on the phenomenon in question. If you would like a glimpse of the other side, you have only to refer to the almost laughable poverty of instinct among German philologists when they approach the Dionysian question. The celebrated Lobeck, especially, who with the venerable assurance of a worm dried up between books, crawled into this world of mysterious states, succeeded in convincing himself that he was scientific, whereas he was simply revoltingly superficial and childish, – Lobeck, with all the pomp of profound erudition, gave us to understand that, as a matter of fact, there was nothing at all in all these curiosities. Truth to tell, the priests may well have communicated not a few things of value to the participators in such orgies; for instance, the fact that wine provokes desire, that man in certain circumstances lives on fruit, that plants bloom in the spring and fade in the autumn. As regards the astounding wealth of rites, symbols and myths which take their origin in the orgy, and with which the world of antiquity is literally smothered, Lobeck finds that it prompts him to a feat of even greater ingenuity than the foregoing phenomenon did. 'The Greeks', he says, (*Aglaophamus*, I. p. 672), 'when they had nothing better to do, laughed, sprang and romped about, or, inasmuch as men also like a change at times, they would sit down, weep and bewail their lot. Others then came up who tried to discover some reason for this strange behaviour; and thus, as an explanation of these habits, there arose an incalculable number of festivals, legends, and myths. On the other hand it was believed that the *farcical performances* which then perchance began to take place on festival days, necessarily formed part of the celebrations, and they were retained as an indispensable part of the ritual.' – This is contemptible nonsense, and no one will take a man like Lobeck seriously for a moment We are very differently affected when we examine the notion 'Hellenic', as Winckelmann and Goethe conceived it, and find it incompatible with that element out of which Dionysian art springs – I speak of orgiasm. In reality I do not doubt that Goethe would have completely excluded any such thing from the potentialities of the Greek soul. *Consequently Goethe did not understand the Greeks.* For it is only in the Dionysian mysteries, in the psychology of the Dionysian state, that the *fundamental fact* of the Hellenic instinct – its 'will to life' – is expressed. What did the Hellene secure himself with these mysteries? *Eternal* life, the eternal recurrence of life; the future promised and hallowed in the past; the triumphant Yea to life despite death and change; real life conceived as the collective prolongation of life through procreation, through the mysteries of sexuality. To the Greeks, the symbol of sex was the most venerated of symbols, the really deep significance of all the piety of antiquity. All the details of the act of procreation, pregnancy and birth gave rise to the loftiest and most solemn feelings. In the doctrine of mysteries, *pain* was pronounced holy: the 'pains of childbirth' sanctify pain in general, – all becoming and all growth, everything that guarantees the future *involves* pain.... In order that there may be eternal joy in creating, in order that the will to life may say Yea to itself in all eternity, the 'pains of childbirth' must also be eternal. All this is what the word Dionysus signifies: I know of no higher symbolism than this Greek symbolism, this symbolism of the Dionysian phenomenon. In it the profoundest instinct of life, the instinct that guarantees the future of life and life eternal, is understood religiously, – the road to life itself, procreation, is pronounced *holy*... It was only Christianity which, with its fundamental resentment against life, made something impure out of sexuality: it flung *filth* at the very basis, the very first condition of our life.

5

The psychology of orgiasm conceived as the feeling of a superabundance of vitality and strength, within the scope of which even pain acts as a *stimulus*, gave me the key to the concept *tragic* feeling, which has been misunderstood not only by Aristotle, but also even more by our pessimists. Tragedy is so far from proving anything in regard to the pessimism of the Greeks, as Schopenhauer maintains, that it ought rather to be considered as the categorical repudiation and *condemnation* thereof. The saying of Yea to life, including even its most strange and most terrible problems, the will to life rejoicing over its own inexhaustibleness in the *sacrifice* of its highest types – this is what I called Dionysian, this is what I divined as the bridge leading to the psychology of the *tragic* poet. Not in order to escape from terror and pity, not to purify one's self of a dangerous passion by discharging it with vehemence – this is how Aristotle understood it – but to be far beyond terror and pity and to be the eternal lust of Becoming itself – that lust which also involves the *lust of destruction*. And with this I once more come into touch with the spot from which I once set out – the 'Birth of Tragedy' was my first transvaluation of all values: with this I again take my stand upon the soil from out of which my will and my capacity spring – I, the last disciple of the philosopher Dionysus, – I, the prophet of eternal recurrence.

THE END.

THE HAMMER SPEAKETH

'Why so hard!' – said the diamond once unto the charcoal; 'are we then not next of kin?'

'Why so soft? O my brethren; this is my question to you. For are ye not – my brothers?

'Why so soft, so servile and yielding? Why are your hearts so fond of denial and self-denial? How is it that so little fate looketh out from your eyes?

'And if ye will not be men of fate and inexorable, how can ye hope one day to conquer with me?

'And if your hardness will not sparkle, cut and divide, how can ye hope one day to create with me?

'For all creators are hard. And it must seem to you blessed to stamp your hand upon millenniums as upon wax, –

Blessed to write upon the will of millenniums as upon brass, – harder than brass, nobler than brass. – Hard through and through is only the noblest.

This new table of values, O my brethren, I set over your heads: Become hard.'

Thus Spake Zarathustra, iii., 29.

THE ANTICHRIST

AN ATTEMPTED CRITICISM OF CHRISTIANITY

PREFACE

This book belongs to the very few. Maybe not one of them is yet alive; unless he be of those who understand my Zarathustra. How *can* I confound myself with those who today already find a hearing? – Only the day after tomorrow belongs to me. Some are born posthumously.

I am only too well aware of the conditions under which a man understands me, and then *necessarily* understands. He must be intellectually upright to the point of hardness, in order even to endure my seriousness and my passion. He must be used to living on mountain-tops – and to feeling the wretched gabble of politics and national egotism *beneath* him. He must have become indifferent; he must never inquire whether truth is profitable or whether it may prove fatal.... Possessing from strength a predilection for questions for which no one has enough courage nowadays; the courage for the *forbidden*; his predestination must be the labyrinth. The experience of seven solitudes. New ears for new music. New eyes for the most remote things. A new conscience for truths which hitherto have remained dumb. And the will to economy on a large scale: to husband his strength and his enthusiasm.... He must honour himself, he must love himself; he must be absolutely free with regard to himself.... Very well then! Such men alone are my readers, my proper readers, my preordained readers: of what account are the rest? – the rest are simply – humanity. – One must be superior to humanity in power, in loftiness of soul, – in contempt.

FRIEDRICH NIETZSCHE.

1

Let us look each other in the face. We are hyperboreans, – we know well enough how far outside the crowd we stand. 'Thou wilt find the way to the Hyperboreans neither by land nor by water': Pindar already knew this much about us. Beyond the north, the ice, and death – *our life, our happiness*.... We discovered happiness; we know the way; we found the way out of thousands of years of labyrinth. Who *else* would have found it? – Not the modern man, surely? – 'I do not know where I am or what I am to do; I am everything that knows not where it is or what to do,' – sighs the modern man. We were made quite ill by *this* modernity, – with its indolent peace, its cowardly compromise, and the whole of the virtuous filth of its yea and nay. This tolerance and *largeur de cœur* which 'forgives' everything because it 'understands' everything, is a Sirocco for us. We prefer to live amid ice than to be breathed upon by modern virtues and other southerly winds!... We were brave enough; we spared neither ourselves nor others: but we were very far from knowing whither to direct our bravery. We were becoming gloomy; people called us fatalists. *Our* fate – it was the abundance, the tension and the storing up of power. We thirsted for thunderbolts and great deeds; we kept at the most respectful distance from the joy of the weakling, from 'resignation'.... Thunder was in our air, that part of nature which we are, became overcast – *for we had no direction*. The formula of our happiness: a yea, a nay, a straight line, a goal.

2

What is good? All that enhances the feeling of power, the Will to Power, and power itself in man. What is bad? – All that proceeds from weakness. What is happiness? – The feeling that power is *increasing*, – that resistance has been overcome.

Not contentment, but more power; not peace at any price, but war; not virtue, but efficiency* (virtue in the Renaissance sense, *virtù*, free from all moralic acid). The weak and the botched shall perish: first principle of our humanity. And they ought even to be helped to perish.

What is more harmful than any vice? – Practical sympathy with all the botched and the weak – Christianity.

---

* The German '*Tüchtigkeit*' has a nobler ring than our word 'efficiency'. – TR.

3

The problem I set in this work is not what will replace mankind in the order of living being! (– Man is an *end* –); but, what type of man must be *reared*, must be *willed*, as having the higher value, as being the most worthy of life and the surest guarantee of the future.

This more valuable type has appeared often enough already: but as a happy accident, as an exception, never as *willed*. He has rather been precisely the most feared; hitherto he has been almost the terrible in itself; – and from out the very fear he provoked there arose the will to rear the type which has how been reared, *attained*: the domestic animal, the gregarious animal, the sick animal man, – the Christian.

4

Mankind does *not* represent a development towards a better, stronger or higher type, in the sense in which this is supposed to occur today. 'Progress' is merely a modern idea – that is to say, a false idea.** The modern European is still far below the European of the Renaissance in value. The process of evolution does not by any means imply elevation, enhancement and increasing strength.

On the other hand isolated and individual cases are continually succeeding in different places on earth, as the outcome of the most different cultures, and in these a *higher type* certainly manifests itself: something which by the side of mankind in general, represents a kind of superman. Such lucky strokes of great success have always been possible and will perhaps always be possible. And even whole races, tribes and nations may in certain circumstances represent such *lucky strokes*.

5

We must not deck out and adorn Christianity: it has waged a deadly war upon this *higher* type of man, it has set a ban upon all the fundamental instincts of this type, and has distilled evil and the devil himself out of these instincts: – the strong man as the typical pariah, the villain. Christianity has sided with everything weak, low, and

---

** *Cf.* Disraeli: 'But enlightened Europe is not happy. Its existence is a fever which it calls progress. Progress to what?' ('Tancred', Book III., Chap, vii.). – TR.

botched; it has made an ideal out of *antagonism* towards all the self-preservative instincts of strong life: it has corrupted even the reason of the strongest intellects, by teaching that the highest values of intellectuality are sinful, misleading and full of temptations. The most lamentable example of this was the corruption of Pascal, who believed in the perversion of his reason through original sin, whereas it had only been perverted by his Christianity.

6

A painful and ghastly spectacle has just risen before my eyes. I tore down the curtain which concealed mankind's *corruption*. This word in my mouth is at least secure from the suspicion that it contains a moral charge against mankind. It is – I would fain emphasise this again – free from moralic acid: to such an extent is this so, that I am most thoroughly conscious of the corruption in question precisely in those quarters in which hitherto people have aspired with most determination to 'virtue' and to 'godliness'. As you have already surmised, I understand corruption in the sense of *decadence*. What I maintain is this, that all the values upon which mankind builds its highest hopes and desires are *decadent* values.

I call an animal, a species, an individual corrupt, when it loses its instincts, when it selects and *prefers* that which is detrimental to it. A history of the 'higher feelings', of 'human ideals' – and it is not impossible that I shall have to write it – would almost explain why man is so corrupt. Life itself, to my mind, is nothing more nor less than the instinct of growth, of permanence, of accumulating forces, of power: where the will to power is lacking, degeneration sets in. My contention is that all the highest values of mankind *lack* this will, – that the values of decline and of *nihilism* are exercising the sovereign power under the cover of the holiest names.

7

Christianity is called the religion of *pity*. – Pity is opposed to the tonic passions which enhance the energy of the feeling of life: its action is depressing. A man loses power when he pities. By means of pity the drain on strength which suffering itself already introduces into the world is multiplied a thousandfold. Through pity, suffering itself becomes infectious; in certain circumstances it may lead to a total loss of life and vital energy, which is absurdly put of proportion to the magnitude of the cause (– the case of the death of the Nazarene). This is the first standpoint; but there is a still more important one. Supposing one measures pity according to the value of the reactions it usually stimulates, its danger to life appears in a much more telling light. On the whole, pity thwarts the law of development which is the law of selection. It preserves that which is ripe for death, it fights in favour of the disinherited and the condemned of life; thanks to the multitude of abortions of all kinds which it maintains in life, it lends life itself a sombre and questionable aspect. People have dared to call pity a virtue (– in every *noble* culture it is considered as a weakness –); people went still further, they exalted it to *the* virtue, the root and origin of all virtues, – but, of course, what must never be forgotten is the fact that this was done from the standpoint of a philosophy which was nihilistic, and on whose shield the device *The Denial of Life* was inscribed. Schopenhauer was right in this respect: by means of pity, life is denied and made *more worthy of denial*, – pity is the *praxis* of Nihilism. I repeat, this depressing and infectious instinct thwarts those instincts which aim at the preservation and enhancement of the value life: by *multiplying* misery quite as much as by preserving all that is miserable, it is the principal agent in promoting decadence, – pity exhorts people to nothing, to *nonentity*! But they do not say '*nonentity*' they say 'Beyond', or 'God', or 'the true life'; or Nirvana, or Salvation, or Blessedness, instead. This innocent rhetoric, which belongs to the realm of the religio-moral idiosyncrasy, immediately appears to be *very much less innocent* if one realises what the tendency is which here tries to drape itself in the mantle of sublime expressions – the tendency of hostility to life. Schopenhauer was hostile to life: that is why he elevated pity to a virtue…. Aristotle, as you know, recognised in pity a morbid and dangerous state, of which it was wise to rid one's self from time to time by a purgative: he regarded tragedy as a purgative. For the sake of the instinct of life, it would certainly seem necessary to find some means of lancing any such morbid and dangerous accumulation of pity, as that which possessed Schopenhauer (and unfortunately the whole of our literary and artistic decadence as well, from St Petersburg to Paris, from Tolstoy to Wagner), if only to make it *burst*…. Nothing is more unhealthy in the midst of our unhealthy modernity, than Christian pity. To be doctors *here*, to be inexorable *here*, to wield the knife effectively *here* – all this is our business, all this is *our* kind of love to our fellows, this is what makes *us* philosophers, us hyperboreans! –

8

It is necessary to state whom we regard as our antithesis: – the theologians, and all those who have the blood of theologians in their veins – the whole of our philosophy.... A man must have had his very nose upon this fatality, or better still he must have experienced it in his own soul; he must almost have perished through it, in order to be unable to treat this matter lightly (the free-spiritedness of our friends the naturalists and physiologists is, in my opinion, a *joke*, – what they lack in these questions is passion, what they lack is having suffered from these questions). This poisoning extends much further than people think: I unearthed the 'arrogant' instinct of the theologian, wherever nowadays people feel themselves idealists wherever, thanks to superior antecedents, they claim the right to rise above reality and to regard it with suspicion.... Like the priest the idealist has every grandiloquent concept in his hand (and not only in his hand!), he wields them all with kindly contempt against the 'understanding', the 'senses', 'honours', 'decent living', 'science'; he regards such things as *beneath* him, as detrimental and seductive forces, upon the face of which, 'the Spirit' moves in pure absoluteness: – as if humility, chastity, poverty, in a word *holiness*, had not done incalculably more harm to life hitherto, than any sort of horror and vice.... Pure spirit is pure falsehood.... As long as the priest, the *professional* denier, calumniator and poisoner of life, is considered as the *highest* kind of man, there can be no answer to the question, what *is* truth? Truth has already been turned topsy-turvy, when the conscious advocate of nonentity and of denial passes as the representative of 'truth'.

9

It is upon this theological instinct that I wage war. I find traces of it everywhere. Whoever has the blood of theologians in his veins, stands from the start in a false and dishonest position to all things. The pathos which grows out of this state, is called *faith*: that is to say, to shut one's eyes once and for all, in order not to suffer at the sight of incurable falsity. People convert this faulty view of all things into a moral, a virtue, a thing of holiness. They endow their distorted vision with a good conscience, – they claim that no *other* point of view is any longer of value, once theirs has been made sacrosanct with the names 'God', 'Salvation', 'Eternity'. I unearthed the instinct of the theologian everywhere: it is the most universal, and actually the most subterranean form of falsity on earth. That which a theologian considers true, *must* of necessity be false: this furnishes almost the criterion of truth. It is his most profound self-preservative instinct which forbids reality ever to attain to honour in any way, or even to raise its voice. Whithersoever the influence of the theologian extends, *valuations* are topsy-turvy, and the concepts 'true' and 'false' have necessarily changed places: that which is most deleterious to life, is here called 'true', that which enhances it, elevates it, says yea to it, justifies it and renders it triumphant, is called 'false'.... If it should happen that theologians, via the 'conscience' either of princes or of the people, stretch out their hand for power, let us not be in any doubt as to what results therefrom each time, namely: – the will to the end, the *nihilistic* will to power....

10

Among Germans I am immediately understood when I say, that philosophy is ruined by the blood of theologians. The Protestant minister is the grandfather of German philosophy, Protestantism itself is the latter's *peccatum originale*. Definition of Protestantism: the partial paralysis of Christianity – and of reason.... One needs only to pronounce the words 'Tübingen Seminary', in order to understand what German philosophy really is at bottom, *i.e.*: theology *in disguise*.... The Swabians are the best liars in Germany, they lie innocently.... Whence came all the rejoicing with which the appearance of Kant was greeted by the scholastic world of Germany, three-quarters of which consist of clergymen's and schoolmasters' sons? Whence came the German conviction, which finds an echo even now, that Kant inaugurated a change for the *better*? The theologian's instinct in the German scholar divined what had once again been made possible.... A back-staircase leading into the old ideal was discovered, the concept 'true world', the concept morality as the *essence* of the world (– those two most vicious errors that have ever existed!), were, thanks to a subtle and wily scepticism, once again, if not demonstrable, at least no longer *refutable*.... Reason, the *prerogative* of reason, does not extend so far.... Out of reality they had made 'appearance'; and an absolutely false world – that of being – had been declared to be reality. Kant's success is merely a theologian's success. Like Luther, and like Leibniz, Kant was one brake the more upon the already squeaky wheel of German uprightness.

11

One word more against Kant as a *moralist*. A virtue *must* be *our* invention, our most personal defence and need: in every other sense it is merely a danger. That which does not constitute a condition of our life, is merely harmful to it: to possess a virtue merely because one happens to respect the concept 'virtue', as Kant would have us do, is pernicious. 'Virtue', 'Duty', 'Goodness in itself', goodness stamped with the character of impersonality and universal validity – these things are mere mental hallucinations, in which decline the final devitalisation of life and Königsbergian Chinadom find expression. The most fundamental laws of preservation and growth, demand precisely the reverse, namely: – that each should discover *his* own virtue, his own categorical imperative. A nation goes to the dogs when it confounds its concept of duty with the general concept of duty. Nothing is more profoundly, more thoroughly pernicious, than every impersonal feeling of duty, than every sacrifice to the Moloch of abstraction. – Fancy no one's having thought Kant's Categorical Imperative *dangerous to life*!... The instinct of the theologist alone took it under its wing! – An action stimulated by the instinct of life, is proved to be a proper action by the happiness that accompanies it: and that nihilist with the bowels of a Christian dogmatist regarded happiness as an *objection*.... What is there that destroys a man more speedily than to work, think, feel, as an automaton of 'duty', without internal promptings, without a profound personal predilection, without joy? This is the recipe *par excellence* of decadence and even of idiocy.... Kant became an idiot – And he was the contemporary of Goethe! This fatal spider was regarded as *the* German philosopher, – is still regarded as such!... I refrain from saying what I think of the Germans.... Did Kant not see in the French Revolution the transition of the State from the inorganic to the *organic* form? Did he not ask himself whether there was a single event on record which could be explained otherwise than as a moral faculty of mankind; so that by means of it, 'mankind's tendency towards good', might be *proved* once and for all? Kant's reply: 'that is the Revolution'. Instinct at fault in anything and everything, hostility to nature as an instinct, German decadence made into philosophy – *that is Kant*!

12

Except for a few sceptics, the respectable type in the history of philosophy, the rest do not know the very first prerequisite of intellectual uprightness. They all behave like females, do these great enthusiasts and animal prodigies, – they regard 'beautiful feelings' themselves as arguments, the 'heaving breast' as the bellows of divinity, and conviction as the *criterion* of truth. In the end, even Kant, with 'Teutonic' innocence, tried to dress this lack of intellectual conscience up in a scientific garb by means of the concept 'practical reason'. He deliberately invented a kind of reason which at times would allow one to dispense with reason, that is to say when 'morality', when the sublime command 'thou shalt', makes itself heard. When one remembers that in almost all nations the philosopher is only a further development of the priestly type, this heirloom of priesthood, this *fraud towards one's self*, no longer surprises one. When a man has a holy life-task, as for instance to improve, save, or deliver mankind, when a man bears God in his breast, and is the mouthpiece of imperatives from another world, – with such a mission he stands beyond the pale of all merely reasonable valuations. He is even sanctified by such a taste, and is already the type of a higher order! What does a priest care about science! He stands too high for that! – And until now the priest has *ruled*! – He it was who determined the concept 'true and false'.

13

Do not let us undervalue the fact that we *ourselves*, we free spirits, are already a 'transvaluation of all values', an incarnate declaration of war against all the old concepts 'true' and 'untrue' and of a triumph over them. The most valuable standpoints are always the last to be found: but the most valuable standpoints are the methods. All the methods and the first principles of our modern scientific procedure, had for years to encounter the profoundest contempt: association with them meant exclusion from the society of decent people – one was regarded as an 'enemy of God', as a scoffer at truth and as 'one possessed'. With one's scientific nature, one belonged to the Chandala. We have had the whole feeling of mankind against us; hitherto their notion of that which ought to be truth, of that which ought to serve the purpose of truth: every 'thou shalt', has been directed against us.... Our objects, our practices, our calm, cautious distrustful manner – everything about us seemed to them absolutely despicable and beneath contempt. After all, it might be asked with some justice, whether the thing which kept mankind blindfold so long, were not an æsthetic taste: what they demanded of truth was a *picturesque* effect, and from the man of science what they expected was that he should make a forcible appeal to their senses. It was our *modesty* which ran counter to their taste so long... And oh! how well they guessed this, did these divine turkey-cocks! –

14

We have altered our standpoint. In every respect we have become more modest. We no longer derive man from the 'spirit', and from the 'godhead'; we have thrust him back among the beasts. We regard him as the strongest animal, because he is the craftiest: one of the results thereof is his intellectuality. On the other hand we guard against the vain pretension, which even here would fain assert itself: that man is the great *arrière pensée* of organic evolution! He is by no means the crown of creation, beside him, every other creature stands at the same stage of perfection.... And even in asserting this we go a little too far; for, relatively speaking, man is the most botched and diseased of animals, and he has wandered furthest from his instincts. Be all this as it may, he is certainly the most *interesting*! As regards animals, Descartes was the first, with really admirable daring, to venture the thought that the beast was *machina*, and the whole of our physiology is endeavouring to prove this proposition. Moreover, logically we do not set man apart, as Descartes did: the extent to which man is understood today goes only so far as he has been understood mechanistically. Formerly man was given 'free will', as his dowry from a higher sphere; nowadays we have robbed him even of will, in view of the fact that no such faculty is any longer known. The only purpose served by the old word 'will', is to designate a result, a sort of individual reaction which necessarily follows upon a host of partly discordant and partly harmonious stimuli: – the will no longer 'effects' or 'moves' anything.... Formerly people thought that man's consciousness, his 'spirit', was a proof of his lofty origin, of his divinity. With the idea of perfecting man, he was conjured to draw his senses inside himself, after the manner of the tortoise, to cut off all relations with terrestrial things, and to divest himself of his mortal shell. Then the most important thing about him, the 'pure spirit', would remain over. Even concerning these things we have improved our standpoint. Consciousness, 'spirit', now seems to us rather a symptom of relative imperfection in the organism, as an experiment, a groping, a misapprehension, an affliction which absorbs an unnecessary quantity of nervous energy. We deny that anything can be done perfectly so long as it is done consciously. 'Pure spirit' is a piece of 'pure stupidity': if we discount the nervous system, the senses and the 'mortal shell', we have miscalculated – that it is all!...

15

In Christianity neither morality nor religion comes in touch at all with reality. Nothing but imaginary *causes* (God, the soul, the ego, spirit, free will – or even non-free will); nothing but imaginary *effects* (sin, salvation, grace, punishment, forgiveness of sins). Imaginary beings are supposed to have intercourse (God, spirits, souls); imaginary natural history (anthropocentric: total lack of the notion 'natural causes'); an imaginary *psychology* (nothing but misunderstandings of self, interpretations of pleasant or unpleasant general feelings; for instance of the states of the *nervus sympathicus*, with the help of the sign language of a religio-moral idiosyncrasy, – repentance, pangs of conscience, the temptation of the devil, the presence of God); an imaginary teleology (the Kingdom of God, the Last Judgment, Everlasting Life). – This purely fictitious world distinguishes itself very unfavourably from the world of dreams: the latter *reflects* reality, whereas the former falsifies, depreciates and denies it. Once the concept 'nature' was taken to mean the opposite of the concept God, the word 'natural' had to acquire the meaning of abominable, – the whole of that fictitious world takes its root in the hatred of nature (reality!), it is the expression of profound discomfiture in the presence of reality.... *But this explains everything.* What is the only kind of man who has reasons for wriggling out of reality by lies? The man who suffers from reality. But in order to suffer from reality one must be a bungled portion of it. The preponderance of pain over pleasure is the *cause* of that fictitious morality and religion: but any such preponderance furnishes the formula for decadences.

16

A criticism of the Christian concept of God inevitably leads to the same conclusion. – A nation that still believes in itself, also has its own God. In him it honours the conditions which enable it to remain uppermost – that is to say, its virtues. It projects its joy over itself, its feeling of power, into a being, to whom it can be thankful for such things. He who is rich, will give of his riches: a proud people requires a God, unto whom it can *sacrifice* things.... Religion, when restricted to these principles, is a form of gratitude. A man is grateful for his own existence; for this he must have a God. – Such a God must be able to benefit and to injure him, he must be able to act the friend and the foe. He must be esteemed for his good as well as for his evil qualities. The monstrous castration of a God by making him a God only of goodness, would lie beyond the pale of the desires of such a community. The evil God is just as urgently needed as the good God: for a people in such a form of society certainly does not owe its existence to toleration and humaneness.... What would be the good of a God who knew nothing of anger, revenge, envy, scorn, craft, and violence? – who had perhaps never experienced the rapturous *ardeurs* of victory and of annihilation? No one would understand such a God: why should one possess him? – Of course, when a people is on the road to ruin; when it feels its belief in a future, its hope of freedom vanishing for ever; when it becomes conscious of submission as the most useful quality, and of the virtues of the submissive as self-preservative measures, then its God must also modify himself. He then becomes a tremulous and unassuming sneak; he counsels 'peace of the soul', the cessation of all hatred, leniency and 'love' even towards friend and foe. He is for ever moralising, he crawls into the heart of every private virtue, becomes a God for everybody, he retires from active service and becomes a Cosmopolitan.... Formerly he represented a people, the strength of a people, everything aggressive and desirous of power lying concealed in the heart of a nation: now he is merely the good God.... In very truth Gods have no other alternative, they are *either* the Will to Power – in which case they are always the Gods of whole nations, – or, on the other hand, the incapacity for power – in which case they necessarily become good.

17

Wherever the Will to Power, no matter in what form, begins to decline, a physiological retrogression, decadence, always supervenes. The godhead of *decadence*, shorn of its masculine virtues and passions is perforce converted into the God of the physiologically degraded, of the weak. Of course they do not call themselves the weak, they call themselves 'the good'.... No hint will be necessary to help you to understand at what moment in history the dualistic fiction of a good and an evil God first became possible. With the same instinct by which the subjugated reduce their God to 'Goodness in itself', they also cancel the good qualities from their conqueror's God; they avenge themselves on their masters by diabolising the latter's God. – The *good God* and the devil as well: – both the abortions of decadence. – How is it possible that we are still so indulgent towards the simplicity of Christian theologians today, as to declare with them that the evolution of the concept God, from the 'God of Israel', the God of a people, to the Christian God, the quintessence of all goodness, marks a *step forward*? – But even Renan does this. As if Renan had a right to simplicity! Why the very contrary stares one in the face. When the prerequisites of *ascending* life, when everything strong, plucky, masterful and proud has been eliminated from the concept of God, and step by step he has sunk down to the symbol of a staff for the weary, of a last straw for all those who are drowning; when he becomes the pauper's God, the sinner's God, the sick man's God *par excellence*, and the attribute 'Saviour', 'Redeemer', remains over as the one essential attribute of divinity: what does such a metamorphosis, such an abasement of the godhead imply? – Undoubtedly, 'the kingdom of God' has thus become larger. Formerly all he had was his people, his 'chosen' people. Since then he has gone travelling over foreign lands, just as his people have done; since then he has never rested anywhere: until one day he felt at home everywhere, the Great Cosmopolitan – until he got the 'greatest number', and half the world on his side. But the God of the 'greatest number', the democrat among gods, did not become a proud heathen god notwithstanding: he remained a Jew, he remained the God of the back streets, the God of all dark corners and hovels, of all the unwholesome quarters of the world!... His universal empire is now as ever a netherworld empire, an infirmary, a subterranean empire, a ghetto-empire.... And he himself is so pale, so weak, so decadent... Even the palest of the pale were able to master him – our friends the metaphysicians, those albinos of thought. They spun their webs around him so long that ultimately he was hypnotised by their movements and himself became a spider, a metaphysician. Thenceforward he once more began spinning the world out of his inner being – *sub specie Spinozæ*, – thenceforward he transfigured himself into something ever thinner and ever more anæmic, became 'ideal', became 'pure spirit', became '*absotutum*' and 'thing-in-itself'.... *The decline and fall of a god*: God became the 'thing-in-itself'.

18

The Christian concept of God – God as the deity of the sick, God as a spider, God as spirit – is one of the most corrupt concepts of God that has ever been attained on earth. Maybe it represents the low-water mark in the evolutionary ebb of the godlike type God degenerated into the *contradiction of life*, instead of being its transfiguration and eternal Yea! With God war is declared on life, nature, and the will to life! God is the formula for every calumny of this world and for every lie concerning a beyond! In God, nonentity is deified, and the will to nonentity is declared holy!

19

The fact that the strong races of Northern Europe did not repudiate the Christian God, certainly does not do any credit to their religious power, not to speak of their taste. They ought to have been able successfully to cope with such a morbid and decrepit offshoot of decadence. And a curse lies on their heads; because they were unable to cope with him: they made illness, decrepitude and contradiction a part of all their instincts – since then they have not *created* any other God! Two thousand years have passed and not a single new God! But still there exists, and as if by right, – like an *ultimum* and *maximum* of god-creating power – the *creator spiritus* in man, this miserable God of Christian monotono-theism! This hybrid creature of decay, nonentity, concept and contradiction, in which all the instincts of decadence, all the cowardices and languors of the soul find their sanction!

20

With my condemnation of Christianity I should not like to have done an injustice to a religion which is related to it and the number of whose followers is even greater; I refer to Buddhism. As nihilistic religions, they are akin – they are religions of decadence – while each is separated from the other in the most extraordinary fashion. For being able to compare them at all, the critic of Christianity is profoundly grateful to Indian scholars. – Buddhism is a hundred times more realistic than Christianity – it is part of its constitutional heritage to be able to face problems objectively and coolly, it is the outcome of centuries of lasting philosophical activity. The concept 'God' was already exploded when it appeared. Buddhism is the only really positive religion to be found in history, even in its epistemology (which is strict phenomenalism) – it no longer speaks of the 'struggle with *sin*' but fully recognising the true nature of reality it speaks of the 'struggle with *pain*'. It already has – and this distinguishes it fundamentally from Christianity, – the self-deception of moral concepts beneath it, – to use my own phraseology, it stands *Beyond Good and Evil*. The two physiological facts upon which it rests and upon which it bestows its attention are: in the first place excessive irritability of feeling, which manifests itself as a refined susceptibility to pain, *and also* as super-spiritualisation, an all-too-lengthy sojourn amid concepts and logical procedures, under the influence of which the personal instinct has suffered in favour of the 'impersonal'. (Both of these states will be known to a few of my readers, the objective ones, who, like myself, will know them from experience.) Thanks to these physiological conditions, a state of depression set in, which Buddha sought to combat by means of hygiene. Against it, he prescribes life in the open, a life of travel; moderation and careful choice in food; caution in regard to all intoxicating liquor, as also in regard to all the passions which tend to create bile and to heat the blood; and he deprecates care either on one's own or on other people's account. He recommends ideas that bring one either peace or good cheer, – he invents means whereby the habit of contrary ideas may be lost. He understands goodness – being good – as promoting health. *Prayer* is out of the question, as is also *asceticism*; there is neither a categorical imperative nor any discipline whatsoever, even within the walls of a monastery (it is always possible to leave it if one wants to). All these things would have been only a means of accentuating the excessive irritability already referred to. Precisely on this account he does not exhort his followers to wage war upon those who do not share their views; nothing is more abhorred in his doctrine than the feeling of revenge, of aversion, and of resentment ('not through hostility doth hostility end': the touching refrain of the whole of Buddhism....) And in this he was right; for it is precisely these passions which are thoroughly unhealthy in view of the principal dietetic object. The mental fatigue which he finds already existent and which expresses itself in excessive 'objectivity' (*i.e.*, the enfeeblement of the individual's interest – loss of ballast and of 'egoism'), he combats by leading the spiritual interests as well imperatively back to the individual. In Buddha's doctrine egoism is a duty: the thing which is above all necessary, *i.e.*, 'how canst thou be rid of suffering' regulates and defines the whole of the spiritual diet (let anyone but think of that Athenian who also declared war upon pure 'scientificality', Socrates, who made a morality out of personal egoism even in the realm of problems).

21

The prerequisites for Buddhism are a very mild climate, great gentleness and liberality in the customs of a people and *no* militarism. The movement must also originate among the higher and even learned classes. Cheerfulness, peace and absence of desire, are the highest of inspirations, and they are *realised*. Buddhism is not a religion in which perfection is merely aspired to: perfection is the normal case. In Christianity all the instincts of the subjugated and oppressed come to the fore: it is the lowest classes who seek their salvation in this religion. Here the pastime, the manner of killing time is to practise the casuistry of sin, self-criticism, and conscience inquisition. Here the ecstasy in the presence of a *powerful being*, called 'god', is constantly maintained by means of prayer; while the highest thing is regarded as unattainable, as a gift, as an act of 'grace' Here plain dealing is also entirely lacking: concealment and the darkened room are Christian. Here the body is despised, hygiene is repudiated as sensual; the church repudiates even cleanliness (the first Christian measure after the banishment of the Moors was the closing of the public baths, of which Cordova alone possessed 270). A certain spirit of cruelty towards one's self and others is also Christian: hatred of all those who do not share one's views; the will to persecute Sombre and exciting ideas are in the foreground; the most coveted states and those which are endowed with the finest names, are really epileptic in their nature; diet is selected in such a way as to favour morbid symptoms and to over-excite the nerves. Christian, too, is the mortal hatred of the earth's rulers, – the 'noble', – and at the same time a sort of concealed and secret competition with them (the subjugated leave the 'body' to their master – all they want is the 'soul'). Christian is the hatred of the intellect, of pride, of courage, freedom, intellectual *libertinage*; Christian is the hatred of the *senses*, of the joys of the senses, of joy in general.

22

When Christianity departed from its native soil, which consisted of the lowest classes, the *submerged masses* of the ancient world, and set forth in quest of power among barbaric nations, it no longer met with exhausted men but inwardly savage and self-lacerating men – the strong but bungled men. Here, dissatisfaction with one's self, suffering through one's self, is not as in the case of Buddhism, excessive irritability and susceptibility to pain, but rather, conversely, it is an inordinate desire for inflicting pain, for a discharge of the inner tension in hostile deeds and ideas. Christianity was in need of *barbaric* ideas and values, in order to be able to master barbarians: such are for instance, the sacrifice of the first-born, the drinking of blood at communion, the contempt of the intellect and of culture; torture in all its forms, sensual and non-sensual; the great pomp of the cult Buddhism is a religion for *senile* men, for races which have become kind, gentle, and over-spiritual, and which feel pain too easily (Europe is not nearly ripe for it yet –); it calls them back to peace and cheerfulness, to a regimen for the intellect, to a certain hardening of the body. Christianity aims at mastering *beasts of prey*; its expedient is to make them *ill*, – to render feeble is the Christian recipe for taming, for 'civilisation'. Buddhism is a religion for the close and exhaustion of civilisation; Christianity does not even find civilisation at hand when it appears, in certain circumstances it lays the foundation of civilisation.

23

Buddhism, I repeat, is a hundred times colder, more truthful, more objective. It no longer requires to justify pain and its susceptibility to suffering by the interpretation of sin – it simply says what it thinks, 'I suffer'. To the barbarian, on the other hand, suffering in itself is not a respectable thing: in order to acknowledge to himself that he suffers, what he requires, in the first place, is an explanation (his instinct directs him more readily to deny his suffering, or to endure it in silence). In his case, the word 'devil' was a blessing: man had an almighty and terrible enemy, – he had no reason to be ashamed of suffering at the hands of such an enemy. –

At bottom there are in Christianity one or two subtleties which belong to the Orient. In the first place it knows that it is a matter of indifference whether a thing be true or not; but that it is of the highest importance that it should be believed to be true. Truth and the belief that something is true: two totally separate worlds of interest, almost *opposite worlds*, the road to the one and the road to the other lie absolutely apart. To be initiated into this fact almost constitutes one a sage in the Orient: the Brahmins understood it thus, so did Plato, and so does every disciple of esoteric wisdom. If for example it give anyone pleasure to believe himself delivered from sin, it is *not* a necessary prerequisite thereto that he should be sinful, but only that he should *feel* sinful. If, however, *faith* is above all necessary, then reason, knowledge, and scientific research must be brought into evil repute: the road to truth becomes the *forbidden* road. – Strong *hope* is a much greater stimulant of life than any single realised joy could be. Sufferers must be sustained by a hope which no actuality can contradict, – and which cannot ever be realised: the hope of another world. (Precisely on account of this power that hope has of making the unhappy linger on, the Greeks regarded it as the evil of evils, as the most *mischievous* evil: it remained behind in Pandora's box.) In order that *love* may be possible, God must be a person. In order that the lowest instincts may also make their voices heard God must be young. For the ardour of the women a beautiful saint, and for the ardour of the men a Virgin Mary has to be pressed into the foreground. All this on condition that Christianity wishes to rule over a certain soil, on which Aphrodisiac or Adonis cults had already determined the *notion* of a cult. To insist upon *chastity* only intensifies the vehemence and profundity of the religious instinct – it makes the cult warmer, more enthusiastic, more soulful. – Love is the state in which man sees things most widely different from what they are. The force of illusion reaches its zenith here, as likewise the sweetening and transfiguring power. When a man is in love he endures more than at other times; he submits to everything. The thing was to discover a religion in which it was possible to love: by this means the worst in life is overcome – it is no longer even seen. – So much for three Christian virtues Faith, Hope, and Charity: I call them the three Christian *precautionary measures*. – Buddhism is too full of aged wisdom, too positivistic to be shrewd in this way.

24

Here I only touch upon the problem of the origin of Christianity. The first principle of its solution reads: Christianity can be understood only in relation to the soil out of which it grew, – it is not a counter-movement against the Jewish instinct, it is the rational outcome of the latter, one step further in its appalling logic. In the formula of the Saviour: 'for Salvation is of the Jews'. – The second principle is: the psychological type of the Galilean is still recognisable, but it was only in a state of utter degeneration (which is at once a distortion and an overloading with foreign features) that he was able to serve the purpose for which he has been used, – namely, as the type of a Redeemer of mankind.

The Jews are the most remarkable people in the history of the world, because when they were confronted with the question of Being or non-Being, with simply uncanny deliberateness, they preferred Being *at any price*: this price was the fundamental *falsification* of all nature, all the naturalness and all the reality, of the inner quite as much as of the outer world. They hedged themselves in behind all those conditions under which hitherto a people has been able to live, has been allowed to live; of themselves they created an idea which was the reverse of natural conditions, – each in turn, they twisted first religion, then the cult, then morality, history and psychology, about in a manner so perfectly hopeless that they were made to *contradict their natural value*. We meet with the same phenomena again, and exaggerated to an incalculable degree, although only as a copy: – the Christian Church as compared with the 'chosen people', lacks all claim to originality. Precisely on this account the Jews are the most *fatal* people in the history of the world: their ultimate influence has falsified mankind to such an extent, that even to this day the Christian can be anti-Semitic in spirit, without comprehending that he himself is the *final consequence of Judaism.*

It was in my 'Genealogy of Morals' that I first gave a psychological exposition of the idea of the antithesis noble and *resentment*-morality, the latter having arisen out of an attitude of negation to the former: but this is Judæo-Christian morality heart and soul. In order to be able to say nay to everything that represents the ascending movement of life, prosperity, power, beauty, and self-affirmation on earth, the instinct of resentment, become genius, had to invent *another* world, from the standpoint of which that *yea-saying* to life appeared as *the* most evil and most abominable thing. From the psychological standpoint the Jewish people are possessed of the toughest vitality. Transplanted amid impossible conditions, with profound self-preservative intelligence, it voluntarily took the side of all the instincts of decadence, – *not* as though dominated by them, but because it detected a power in them by means of which it could assert itself *against* 'the world'. The Jews are the opposite of all *decadents*: they have been forced to represent them to the point of illusion, and with a *non plus ultra* of histrionic genius, they have known how to set themselves at the head of all decadent movements (St Paul and Christianity for instance), in order to create something from them which is stronger than every party *saying yea to life*. For the category of men which aspires to power in Judaism and Christianity, – that is to say, for the sacerdotal class, decadence is but a *means*; this category of men has a vital interest in making men sick, and in turning the notions 'good' and 'bad', 'true' and 'false', upside down in a manner which is not only dangerous to life, but also slanders it.

25

The history of Israel is invaluable as the typical history of every *denaturalization* of natural values: let me point to five facts which relate thereto. Originally, and above all in the period of the kings, even Israel's attitude to all things was the *right* one – that is to say, the natural one. Its Jehovah was the expression of its consciousness of power, of its joy over itself, of its hope for itself: victory and salvation were expected from him, through him it was confident that nature would give what a people requires – above all rain. Jehovah is the God of Israel, and *consequently* the God of justice: this is the reasoning of every people which is in the position of power, and which has a good conscience in that position. In the solemn cult both sides of this self-affirmation of a people find expression: it is grateful for the great strokes of fate by means of which it became uppermost; it is grateful for the regularity in the succession of the seasons and for all good fortune in the rearing of cattle and in the tilling of the soil. – This state of affairs remained the ideal for some considerable time, even after it had been swept away in a deplorable manner by anarchy from within and the Assyrians from without. But the people still retained, as their highest desideratum, that vision of a king who was a good soldier and a severe judge; and he who retained it most of all was that typical prophet (– that is to say, critic and satirist of the age), Isaiah. – But all hopes remained unrealised. The old God was no longer able to do what he had done formerly. He ought to have been dropped. What happened? The idea of him was changed, – the idea of him was denaturalised: this was the price they paid for retaining him. – Jehovah, the God of 'Justice', – is no longer one with Israel, no longer the expression of a people's sense of dignity: he is only a god on certain conditions…. The idea of him becomes a weapon in the hands of priestly agitators who henceforth interpret all happiness as a reward, all unhappiness as a punishment for disobedience to God, for 'sin': that most fraudulent method of interpretation which arrives at a so-called 'moral order of the Universe', by means of which the concept 'cause' and 'effect' is turned upside down. Once natural causation has been swept out of the world by reward and punishment, a causation *hostile to nature* becomes necessary; whereupon all the forms of unnaturalness follow. A God who *demands*, – in the place of a God who helps, who advises, who is at bottom only a name for every happy inspiration of courage and of self-reliance…. Morality is no longer the expression of the conditions of life and growth, no longer the most fundamental instinct of life, but it has become abstract, it has become the opposite of life, – morality as the fundamental perversion of the imagination, as the 'evil eye' for all things. What is Jewish morality, what is Christian morality? Chance robbed of its innocence; unhappiness polluted with the idea of 'sin'; well-being interpreted as a danger, as a 'temptation'; physiological indisposition poisoned by means of the cankerworm of conscience….

26

The concept of God falsified; the concept of morality falsified: but
the Jewish priesthood did not stop at this. No use could be made of
the whole *history* of Israel, therefore it must go! These priests
accomplished that miracle of falsification, of which the greater part
of the Bible is the document: with unparalleled contempt and in the
teeth of all tradition and historical facts, they interpreted their own
people's past in a religious manner, – that is to say, they converted it
into a ridiculous mechanical process of salvation, on the principle that
all sin against Jehovah led to punishment, and that all pious worship
of Jehovah led to reward. We would feel this shameful act of historical
falsification far more poignantly if the ecclesiastical interpretation of
history through millenniums had not blunted almost all our sense for
the demands of uprightness in *historicis*. And the church is seconded
by the philosophers: *the lie* of 'a moral order of the universe' permeates
the whole development even of more modern philosophy. What does
a 'moral order of the universe' mean? That once and for all there is
such a thing as a will of God which determines what man has to do
and what he has to leave undone; that the value of a people or of an
individual is measured according to how much or how little the one
or the other obeys the will of God; that in the destinies of a people
or of an individual, the will of God shows itself dominant, that is to
say it punishes or rewards according to the degree of obedience. In
the place of this miserable falsehood, *reality* says: a parasitical type
of man, who can flourish only at the cost of all the healthy elements
of life, the priest abuses the name of God: he calls that state of affairs
in which the priest determines the value of things 'the Kingdom of
God'; he calls the means whereby such a state of affairs is attained
or maintained, 'the Will of God'; with cold-blooded cynicism he
measures peoples, ages and individuals according to whether they
favour or oppose the ascendancy of the priesthood. Watch him at
work: in the hands of the Jewish priesthood the Augustan Age in the
history of Israel became an age of decline; the exile, the protracted
misfortune transformed itself into eternal *punishment* for the Augustan
Age – that age in which the priest did not yet exist. Out of the mighty
and thoroughly free-born figures of the history of Israel, they made,
according to their requirements, either wretched bigots and hypocrites,
or 'godless ones': they simplified the psychology of every great event

to the idiotic formula 'obedient or disobedient to God'. – A step further: the 'Will of God,' that is to say the self-preservative measures of the priesthood, must be known – to this end a 'revelation' is necessary. In plain English: a stupendous literary fraud becomes necessary, 'holy scriptures' are discovered, – and they are published abroad with all hieratic pomp, with days of penance and lamentations over the long state of 'sin'. The 'Will of God' has long stood firm: the whole of the trouble lies in the fact that the 'Holy Scriptures' have been discarded.... Moses was already the 'Will of God' revealed.... What had happened? With severity and pedantry, the priest had formulated once and for all – even to the largest and smallest contributions that were to be paid to him (– not forgetting the daintiest portions of meat; for the priest is a consumer of beef-steaks) – *what he wanted*, 'what the Will of God was'.... Hence-forward everything became so arranged that the priests were *indispensable everywhere*. At all the natural events of life, at birth, at marriage, at the sick-bed, at death, – not to speak of the sacrifice ('the meal'), – the holy parasite appears in order to denaturalise, or in his language, to 'sanctify', everything.... For this should be understood: every natural custom, every natural institution (the State, the administration of justice, marriage, the care of the sick and the poor), every demand inspired by the instinct of life, in short everything that has a value in itself, is rendered absolutely worthless and even dangerous through the parasitism of the priest (or of the 'moral order of the universe'): a sanction after the fact is required, – a *power which imparts value* is necessary, which in so doing says, nay to nature, and which by this means alone *creates* a valuation.... The priest depreciates and desecrates nature: it is only at this price that he exists at all. – Disobedience to God, that is to say, to the priest, to the 'law', now receives the name of 'sin'; the means of 'reconciling one's self with God' are of course of a nature which render subordination to the priesthood all the more fundamental: the priest alone is able to 'save'.... From the psychological standpoint, in every society organised upon a hieratic basis, 'sins' are indispensable: they are the actual weapons of power, the priest lives upon sins, it is necessary for him that people should 'sin'.... Supreme axiom: 'God forgiveth him that repenteth' – in plain English: *him that submitteth himself to the priest.*

27

Christianity grew out of an utterly *false* soil, in which all nature, every natural value, every *reality* had the deepest instincts of the ruling class against it; it was a form of deadly hostility to reality which has never been surpassed. The 'holy people' which had retained only priestly values and priestly names for all things, and which, with a logical consistency that is terrifying, had divorced itself from everything still powerful on earth as if it were 'unholy', 'worldly', 'sinful', – this people created a final formula for its instinct which was consistent to the point of self-suppression; as *Christianity* it denied even the last form of reality, the 'holy people', the 'chosen people', *Jewish* reality itself. The case is of supreme interest: the small insurrectionary movement christened with the name of Jesus of Nazareth, is the Jewish instinct *over again*, – in other words, it is the sacerdotal instinct which can no longer endure the priest as a fact; it is the discovery of a kind of life even more fantastic than the one previously conceived, a vision of life which is even more unreal than that which the organisation of a church stipulates. Christianity denies the church.[*]

I fail to see against whom was directed the insurrection of which rightly or *wrongly* Jesus is understood to have been the promoter, if it were not directed against the Jewish church, – the word 'church' being used here in precisely the same sense in which it is used today. It was an insurrection against the 'good and the just', against the 'prophets of Israel', against the hierarchy of society – not against the latter's corruption, but against caste, privilege, order, formality. It was the lack of faith in 'higher men', it was a 'Nay' uttered against everything that was tinctured with the blood of priests and theologians. But the hierarchy which was set in question if only temporarily by this movement, formed the construction of piles upon which, alone, the Jewish people was able to subsist in the midst of the 'waters'; it was that people's *last* chance of survival wrested from the world at enormous pains, the *residuum* of its political autonomy: to attack this construction was tantamount to attacking the most profound

---

[*] It will be seen from this that in spite of Nietzsche's ruthless criticism of the priests, he draws a sharp distinction between Christianity and the Church. As the latter still contained elements of order, it was more to his taste than the denial of authority characteristic of real Christianity. – TR.

popular instinct, the most tenacious national will to live that has ever existed on earth. This saintly anarchist who called the lowest of the low, the outcasts and 'sinners', the Chandala of Judaism, to revolt against the established order of things (and in language which, if the gospels are to be trusted, would get one sent to Siberia even today) – this man was a political criminal in so far as political criminals were possible in a community so absurdly non-political. This brought him to the cross: the proof of this is the inscription found thereon. He died for *his* sins – and no matter how often the contrary has been asserted there is absolutely nothing to show that he died for the sins of others.

28

As to whether he was conscious of this contrast, or whether he was merely *regarded* as such, is quite another question. And here, alone, do I touch upon the problem of the psychology of the Saviour. – I confess there are few books which I have as much difficulty in reading as the gospels. These difficulties are quite different from those which allowed the learned curiosity of the German mind to celebrate one of its most memorable triumphs. Many years have now elapsed since I, like every young scholar, with the sage conscientiousness of a refined philologist, relished the work of the incomparable Strauss. I was then twenty years of age; now I am too serious for that sort of thing. What do I care about the contradictions of 'tradition'? How can saintly legends be called 'tradition' at all! The stories of saints constitute the most ambiguous literature on earth: to apply the scientific method to them, *when there are no other documents to hand*, seems to me to be a fatal procedure from the start – simply learned fooling.

29

The point that concerns me is the psychological type of the Saviour. This type might be contained in the gospels, in spite of the gospels, and however much it may have been mutilated, or overladen with foreign features: just as that of Francis of Assisi is contained in his legends in spite of his legends. It is not a question of the truth concerning what he has done, what he has said, and how he actually died; but whether his type may still be conceived in any way, whether it has been handed down to us at all? – The attempts which to my knowledge have been made to read the *history* of a 'soul' out of the gospels, seem to me to point only to disreputable levity in psychological matters. M. Renan, that buffoon *in psychologies*, has contributed the two most monstrous ideas imaginable to the explanation of the type of Jesus: the idea of the *genius* and the idea of the hero (*'héros'*). But if there is anything thoroughly unevangelical surely it is the idea of the hero. It is precisely the reverse of all struggle, of all consciousness of taking part in the fight, that has become instinctive here: the inability to resist is here converted into a morality ('resist not evil', the profoundest sentence in the whole of the gospels, their key in a certain sense), the blessedness of peace, of gentleness, of not *being able* to be an enemy. What is the meaning of 'glad tidings'? – True life, eternal life has been found – it is not promised, it is actually here, it is in *you*; it is life in love, in love free from all selection or exclusion, free from all distance. Everybody is the child of God – Jesus does not by any means claim anything for himself alone, – as the child of God everybody is equal to everybody else…. Fancy making Jesus a *hero*! – And what a tremendous misunderstanding the word 'genius' is! Our whole idea of 'spirit', which is a civilised idea, could have had no meaning whatever in the world in which Jesus lived. In the strict terms of the physiologist, a very different word ought to be used here…. We know of a condition of morbid irritability of the sense of *touch*, which recoils shuddering from every kind of contact, and from every attempt at grasping a solid object. Any such physiological *habitus* reduced to its ultimate logical conclusion, becomes an instinctive hatred of all reality, a flight into the 'intangible', into the 'incomprehensible'; a repugnance to all formulæ, to every notion of time and space, to everything that is established such as customs, institutions, the church; a feeling at one's ease in a world in which no sign of reality is any longer visible, a merely 'inner' world, a 'true' world, an 'eternal' world…. 'The Kingdom of God is within you'…

30

The instinctive hatred of reality is the outcome of an extreme susceptibility to pain and to irritation, which can no longer endure to be 'touched' at all, because every sensation strikes too deep.

The instinctive exclusion of all aversion, of all hostility, of all boundaries and distances in feeling, is the outcome of an extreme susceptibility to pain and to irritation, which regards all resistance, all compulsory resistance as insufferable *anguish* (that is to say, as harmful, as *deprecated* by the self-preservative instinct), and which knows blessedness (happiness) only when it is no longer obliged to offer resistance to anybody, either evil or detrimental, – love as the only ultimate possibility of life....

These are the two *physiological realities* upon which and out of which the doctrine of salvation has grown. I call them a sublime further development of hedonism, upon a thoroughly morbid soil. Epicureanism, the pagan theory of salvation, even though it possessed a large proportion of Greek vitality and nervous energy, remains the most closely related to the above. Epicurus was a *typical* decadent: and I was the first to recognise him as such. – The terror of pain, even of infinitely slight pain – such a state cannot possibly help culminating in a *religion* of love....

31

I have given my reply to the problem in advance. The prerequisite thereto was the admission of the fact that the type of the Saviour has reached us only in a very distorted form. This distortion in itself is extremely feasible: for many reasons a type of that kind could not be pure, whole, and free from additions. The environment in which this strange figure moved, must have left its mark upon him, and the history, the *destiny* of the first Christian communities must have done so to a still greater degree. Thanks to that destiny, the type must have been enriched retrospectively with features which can be interpreted only as serving the purposes of war and of propaganda. That strange and morbid world into which the gospels lead us – a world which seems to have been drawn from a Russian novel, where the scum and dross of society, diseases of the nerves and 'childish' imbecility seem to have given each other rendezvous – must in any case have *coarsened* the type: the first disciples especially must have translated an existence conceived entirely in symbols and abstractions into their own crudities, in order at least to be able to understand something about it, – for them the type existed only after it had been cast in a more familiar mould.... The prophet, the Messiah, the future judge, the teacher of morals, the thaumaturgist, John the Baptist – all

these were but so many opportunities of misunderstanding the type....
Finally, let us not under-rate the *proprium* of all great and especially
sectarian veneration: very often it effaces from the venerated object,
all the original and frequently painfully unfamiliar traits and
idiosyncrasies – *it does not even see them*. It is greatly to be deplored
that no Dostoevsky lived in the neighbourhood of this most interesting
decadent – I mean someone who would have known how to feel the
poignant charm of such a mixture of the sublime, the morbid, and
the childlike. Finally, the type, as an example of decadence, may
actually have been extraordinarily multifarious and contradictory:
this, as a possible alternative, is not to be altogether ignored. Albeit,
everything seems to point away from it; for, precisely in this case,
tradition would necessarily have been particularly true and objective:
whereas we have reasons for assuming the reverse. Meanwhile a
yawning chasm of contradiction separates the mountain, lake, and
pastoral preacher, who strikes us as a Buddha on a soil only very
slightly Hindu, from that combative fanatic, the mortal enemy of
theologians and priests, whom Renan's malice has glorified as *'le
grand maître en ironie'*. For my part, I do not doubt but what the
greater part of this venom (and even of *esprit*) was inoculated into
the type of the Master only as the outcome of the agitated condition
of Christian propaganda. For we have ample reasons for knowing
the unscrupulousness of all sectarians when they wish to contrive
their own *apology* out of the person of their master. When the first
Christian community required a discerning, wrangling, quarrelsome,
malicious and hair-splitting theologian, to oppose other theologians,
it created its 'God' according to its needs; just as it did not hesitate
to put upon his lips those utterly unevangelical ideas of 'his second
coming', the 'last judgment', – ideas with which it could not then
dispense, – and every kind of expectation and promise which
happened to be current.

32

I can only repeat that I am opposed to the importation of the fanatic
into the type of the Saviour: the word *'impérieux'*, which Renan uses,
in itself annuls the type. The 'glad tidings' are simply that there are
no longer any contradictions, that the Kingdom of Heaven is for the
children; the faith which raises its voice here is not a faith that has

been won by a struggle, – it is to hand, it was there from the beginning, it is a sort of spiritual return to childishness. The case of delayed and undeveloped puberty in the organism, as the result of degeneration is at least familiar to physiologists. A faith of this sort does not show anger, it does not blame, neither does it defend itself: it does not bring 'the sword', – it has no inkling of how it will one day establish feuds between man and man. It does not demonstrate itself, either by miracles, or by reward and promises, or yet through the scriptures: it is in itself at every moment its own miracle, its own reward, its own proof, its own Kingdom of God'. This faith cannot be formulated – it lives, it guards against formulas. The accident of environment, of speech, of preparatory culture, certainly determines a particular series of conceptions: early Christianity deals only in Judæo-Semitic conceptions (the eating and drinking at the last supper form part of these, – this idea which like everything Jewish has been abused so maliciously by the church). But one should guard against seeing anything more than a language of signs, semiotics, an opportunity for parables in all this. The very fact that no word is to be taken literally, is the only condition on which this anti-realist is able to speak at all. Among Indians he would have made use of the ideas of Sankhyara, among Chinese, those of Lao-tze – and would not have been aware of any difference. With a little terminological laxity Jesus might be called a 'free spirit' – he cares not a jot for anything that is established: the word *killeth*, everything fixed *killeth*. The idea, *experience*, 'life' as he alone knows it, is, according to him, opposed to every kind of word, formula, law, faith and dogma. He speaks only of the innermost things: 'life' or 'truth', or 'light', is his expression for the innermost thing – everything else, the whole of reality, the whole of nature, language even, has only the value of a sign, of a simile for him. – It is of paramount importance not to make any mistake at this point, however great may be the temptation thereto that lies in Christian – I mean to say, ecclesiastical prejudice. Any such essential symbolism stands beyond the pale of all religion, all notions of cult, all history, all natural science, all experience of the world, all knowledge, all politics, all psychology, all books and all art – for his 'wisdom' is precisely the complete ignorance* of the existence of such things. He has not even heard speak of *culture*, he does not require to oppose it, – he does not deny it…. The same holds good of the state, of the whole of civil and social order, of work and of war – he never had any reason to deny the world, he had not the vaguest notion of the ecclesiastical concept 'the world'.... Denying is precisely what was quite impossible to him. – Dialectic is also quite absent, as likewise the idea that any faith, any 'truth' can be proved by argument (his proofs are inner 'lights', inward feelings of happiness and self-affirmation, a host of 'proofs of power'). Neither can such a doctrine contradict, it does not even realise the fact that there are or can be other doctrines, it is absolutely incapable of imagining a contrary judgment.... Wherever it encounters such things, from a feeling of profound sympathy it bemoans such 'blindness', – for it sees the 'light', – but it raises no objections.

33

The whole psychology of the 'gospels' lacks the concept of guilt and punishment, as also that of reward. 'Sin', any sort of aloofness between God and man, is done away with, – *this is precisely what constitutes the 'glad tidings'*. Eternal bliss is not promised, it is not bound up with certain conditions; it is the only reality – the rest consists only of signs wherewith to speak about it....

The results of such a state project themselves into a new practice of life, the actual evangelical practice. It is not a 'faith' which distinguishes the Christians: the Christian acts, he distinguishes himself by means of a *different* mode of action. He does not resist his enemy either by words or in his heart He draws no distinction between foreigners and natives, between Jews and Gentiles ('the neighbour' really means the co-religionist, the Jew). He is angry with no one, he despises no one. He neither shows himself at the tribunals nor does he acknowledge any of their claims ('Swear not at all'). He never under any circumstances divorces his wife, even when her infidelity has been proved. – All this is at bottom one principle, it is all the outcome of one instinct. –

The life of the Saviour was naught else than this practice, – neither was his death. He no longer required any formulæ, any rites for his relations with God – not even prayer. He has done with all the Jewish teaching of repentance and of atonement; he alone knows the mode

---

* '*reine Thorheit*' in the German text, referring once again to Parsifal. – TR.

of life which makes one feel 'divine', 'saved', 'evangelical', and at all times a 'child of God'. *Not* 'repentance', *not* 'prayer and forgiveness' are the roads to God: the *evangelical mode of life alone* leads to God, it *is* 'God'. – That which the gospels abolished was the Judaism of the concepts 'sin', 'forgiveness of sin', 'faith', 'salvation through faith', – the whole doctrine of the Jewish church was denied by the 'glad tidings'.

The profound instinct of how one must live in order to feel 'in Heaven', in order to feel 'eternal', while in every other respect one feels by no means 'in Heaven': this alone is the psychological reality of 'Salvation'. – A new life and *not* a new faith....

34

If I understand anything at all about this great symbolist, it is this that he regarded only *inner* facts as facts, as 'truths', – that he understood the rest, everything natural, temporal, material and historical, only as signs, as opportunities for parables. The concept 'the Son of Man', is not a concrete personality belonging to history, anything individual and isolated, but an 'eternal' fact, a psychological symbol divorced from the concept of time. The same is true, and in the highest degree, of the *God* of this typical symbolist, of the 'Kingdom of God', of the 'Kingdom of Heaven', and of the 'Sonship of God'. Nothing is more un-Christlike than the *ecclesiastical crudity* of a personal God, of a Kingdom of God that is coming, of a 'Kingdom of Heaven' beyond, of a 'Son of God' as the second person of the Trinity. All this, if I may be forgiven the expression, is as fitting as a square peg in a round hole – and oh! what a hole! – the gospels: a *world-historic* cynicism in the scorn of symbols.... But what is meant by the signs 'Father' and 'Son', is of course obvious – not to everybody, I admit: with the word 'Son', *entrance* into the feeling of the general transfiguration of all things (beatitude) is expressed, with the word 'Father', *this feeling itself* the feeling of eternity and of perfection. – I blush to have to remind you of what the Church has done with this symbolism: has it not set an Amphitryon story at the threshold of the Christian 'faith'? And a dogma of immaculate conception into the bargain?... *But by so doing it defiled conception.* –

The 'Kingdom of Heaven' is a state of the heart – not something which exists 'beyond this earth' or comes to you 'after death'. The whole idea of natural death is lacking in the gospels. Death is not a bridge, not a means of access: it is absent because it belongs to quite a different and merely apparent world the only use of which is to furnish signs, similes. The 'hour of death' is not a Christian idea – the hour', time in general, physical life and its crises do not exist for the messenger of 'glad tidings'…. The 'Kingdom of God' is not some thing that is expected; it has no yesterday nor any day after tomorrow, it is not going to come in a 'thousand years' – it is an experience of a human heart; it is everywhere, it is nowhere….

35

This 'messenger of glad tidings' died as he lived and as he taught – *not* in order 'to save mankind', but in order to show how one ought to live. It was a mode of life that he bequeathed to mankind: his behaviour before his judges, his attitude towards his executioners, his accusers, and all kinds of calumny and scorn, – his demeanour on the *cross*. He offers no resistance; he does not defend his rights; he takes no step to ward off the most extreme consequences, he does more, – he provokes them. And he prays, suffers and loves with those, in those, who treat him ill…. *Not* to defend one's self, *not* to show anger, not to hold anyone responsible…. But to refrain from resisting even the evil one, – to *love* him….

36

Only we spirits that have *become free*, possess the necessary condition for understanding something which nineteen centuries have misunderstood, – that honesty which has become an instinct and a passion in us, and which wages war upon the 'holy lie' with even more vigour than upon every other lie…. Mankind was unspeakably far from our beneficent and cautious neutrality, from that discipline of the mind, which, alone, renders the solution of such strange and subtle things possible: at all times, with shameless egoism, all that people sought was their *own* advantage in these matters, the Church was built up out of contradiction to the gospel….

Whoever might seek for signs pointing to the guiding fingers of an ironical deity behind the great comedy of existence, would find no small argument in the *huge note of interrogation* that is called Christianity. The fact that mankind is on its knees before the reverse of that which formed the origin, the meaning and the *rights* of the gospel; the fact that, in the idea 'Church', precisely that is pronounced holy which the 'messenger of glad tidings' regarded as *beneath* him, as *behind* him – one might seek in vain for a more egregious example of *world-historic* irony. –

37

Our age is proud of its historical sense: how could it allow itself to be convinced of the nonsensical idea that at the beginning Christianity consisted only of the *clumsy fable of the thaumaturgist and of the Saviour*, and that all its spiritual and symbolic side was only developed later? On the contrary: the history of Christianity – from the death on the cross onwards – is the history of a gradual and ever coarser misunderstanding of an original symbolism. With every extension of Christianity over ever larger and ruder masses, who were ever less able to grasp its first principles, the need of *vulgarising and barbarising it* increased proportionately – it absorbed the teachings and rites of all the *subterranean* cults of the *imperium Romanum*, as well as the nonsense of every kind of morbid reasoning. The fatal feature of Christianity lies in the necessary fact that its faith had to become as morbid, base and vulgar as the needs to which it had to minister were morbid, base and vulgar. *Morbid barbarism* at last braces itself together for power in the form of the Church – the Church, this deadly hostility to all honesty, to all loftiness of the soul, to all discipline of the mind, to all frank and kindly humanity. – *Christian* and *noble* values: only we spirits *who have become free* have re-established this contrast in values which is the greatest that has ever existed on earth! –

38

I cannot, at this point, stifle a sigh. There are days when I am visited by a feeling blacker than the blackest melancholy – *the contempt of man*. And in order that I may leave you in no doubt as to what I despise, *whom* I despise: I declare that it is the man of today, the man with whom I am fatally contemporaneous. The man of today, I am asphyxiated by his foul breath…. Towards the past, like all knights of knowledge, I am profoundly tolerant, – that is to say, I exercise a sort of *generous* self-control: with gloomy caution I pass through whole millennia of this mad-house world, and whether it be called 'Christianity', 'Christian Faith', or 'Christian Church', I take care not to hold mankind responsible for its mental disorders. But my feeling suddenly changes, and vents itself the moment I enter the modern age, *our* age. Our age *knows*.... That which formerly was merely morbid, is now positively indecent It is indecent nowadays to be a Christian. *And it is here that my loathing begins.* I look about me: not a word of what was formerly known as 'truth' has remained standing; we can no longer endure to hear a priest even pronounce the word 'truth'. Even he who makes but the most modest claims upon truth, *must* know at present, that a theologian, a priest, or a pope, not only errs but actually *lies*, with every word that he utters, – and that he is no longer able to lie from 'innocence', from 'ignorance'. Even the priest knows quite as well as everybody else does that there is no longer any 'God', any 'sinner' or any 'Saviour', and that 'free will', and 'a moral order of the universe' are *lies*. Seriousness, the profound self-conquest of the spirit no longer allows anyone to be *ignorant* about this.... All the concepts of the Church have been revealed in their true colours – that is to say, as the most vicious frauds on earth, calculated to *depreciate* nature and all natural values. The priest himself has been recognised as what he is – that is to say, as the most dangerous kind of parasite, as the actual venomous spider of existence.... At present we know, our *conscience* knows, the real value of the gruesome inventions which the priests and the Church have made, and *what end they served*. By means of them that state of self-profanation on the part of man has been attained, the sight of which makes one heave. The concepts 'Beyond', 'Last Judgment', 'Immortality of the Soul', the 'soul' itself, are merely so many instruments of torture, so many systems of cruelty, on the strength of which the priest became and remained master.... Everybody knows this, *and nevertheless everything remains as it was*. Whither has the last shred of decency, of self-respect gone, if nowadays even our statesmen – a body of men who are otherwise so unembarrassed, and such thorough anti-Christians in deed – still declare themselves Christians and still flock to communion?*.... Fancy a prince at the head of his legions, magnificent as the expression of the egoism and self-exaltation of his people, – but *shameless* enough to acknowledge himself a Christian!... What then does Christianity deny? What does it call 'world'? 'The world' to Christianity means that a man is a soldier, a judge, a patriot, that he defends himself, that he values his honour, that he desires his own advantage, that he is *proud*.... The conduct of every moment, every instinct, every valuation that leads to a deed, is at present anti-Christian: what an *abortion of falsehood* modern man must be, in order to be able *without a blush* still to call himself a Christian!

39

I will retrace my steps, and will tell you the *genuine* history of Christianity. – The very word 'Christianity' is a misunderstanding – truth to tell, there never was more than one Christian, and he *died* on the Cross. The 'gospel' *died* on the cross. That which thenceforward was called 'gospel' was the reverse of that 'gospel' that Christ had lived: it was 'evil tidings', a *dysangel*. It is false to the point of nonsense to see in 'faith', in the faith in salvation through Christ, the distinguishing trait of the Christian: the only thing that is Christian is the Christian mode of existence, a life such as he led who died on the Cross.... To this day a life of this kind is still possible; for certain men, it is even necessary: genuine, primitive Christianity will be possible in all ages.... *Not* a faith, but a course of action, above all a course of inaction, non-interference, and a different life.... States of consciousness, any sort of faith, a holding of certain things for true, as every psychologist knows, are indeed of absolutely no consequence, and are only of fifth-rate importance compared with the value of the instincts: more exactly, the whole concept of intellectual causality is false. To reduce the fact of being a Christian, or of Christianity, to a holding of something for true, to a mere phenomenon of consciousness, is tantamount to denying Christianity. *In fact there have never been any Christians*. The 'Christian', he who for two thousand years has been called a Christian, is merely a psychological misunderstanding of self. Looked at more closely, there ruled in him, *notwithstanding* all his faith, only instincts – and *what instincts*! – 'Faith' in all ages, as for instance in the case of Luther, has always been merely a cloak, a pretext, a *screen*, behind which the instincts

---

* This applies apparently to Bismarck, the forger of the Ems telegram and a sincere Christian. – TR.

played their game, – a prudent form of *blindness* in regard to the dominion of *certain* instincts. 'Faith' I have already characterised as a piece of really Christian cleverness; for people have always spoken of 'faith' and acted according to their instincts.... In the Christian's world of ideas there is nothing which even touches reality: but I have already recognised in the instinctive hatred of reality the actual motive force, the only driving power at the root of Christianity. What follows therefrom? That here, even *in psychologicis*, error is fundamental – that is to say capable of determining the spirit of things, – that is to say, *substance*. Take one idea away from the whole, and put one realistic fact in its stead, – and the whole of Christianity tumbles into nonentity! – Surveyed from above, this strangest of all facts – a religion not only dependent upon error, but inventive and showing signs of genius only in those errors which are dangerous and which poison life and the human heart – remains a *spectacle for gods*, for those gods who are at the same time philosophers and whom I met for instance in those celebrated dialogues on the island of Naxos. At the moment when they get rid of their *loathing (and we do as well!)*, they will be thankful for the spectacle the Christians have offered: the wretched little planet called Earth perhaps deserves on account of *this* curious case alone, a divine glance, and divine interest.... Let us not therefore underestimate the Christians: the Christian, false *to the point of innocence in falsity*, is far above the apes – in regard to the Christians a certain well-known theory of Descent becomes a mere good-natured compliment.

40

The fate of the gospel was decided at the moment of the death, – it hung on the 'cross'.... It was only death, this unexpected and ignominious death; it was only the cross which as a rule was reserved simply for the *canaille*, – only this appalling paradox which confronted the disciples with the actual riddle: *Who was that? what was that?* – The state produced by the excited and profoundly wounded feelings of these men, the suspicion that such a death might imply the *refutation* of their cause, and the terrible note of interrogation: 'why precisely thus?' will be understood only too well. In this case everything *must* be necessary, everything must have meaning, a reason, the highest reason. The love of a disciple admits of no such thing as accident. Only then did the chasm yawn: 'who has killed him?' 'who was his natural enemy?' – this question rent the firmament like a flash of lightning. Reply: *dominant* Judaism, its ruling class. Thenceforward the disciple felt himself in revolt *against* established order; he understood Jesus, after the fact, as one in *revolt against established order*. Heretofore this warlike, this nay-saying and nay-doing feature in Christ had been lacking; nay more, he was its contradiction. The small primitive community had obviously understood *nothing* of the principal factor of all, which was the example of freedom and of superiority to every form of *resentment* which lay in this way of dying. And this shows how little they understood him altogether! At bottom Jesus could not have desired anything else by his death than to give the strongest public *example* and *proof* of his doctrine.... But his disciples were very far from *forgiving* this death – though if they had done so it would have been in the highest sense evangelical on their part, – neither were they prepared, with a gentle and serene calmness of heart, to *offer* themselves for a similar death.... Precisely the most unevangelical feeling, *revenge*, became once more ascendant. It was impossible for the cause to end with this death: 'compensation' and 'judgment' were required (and forsooth, what could be more unevangelical than 'compensation', 'punishment', 'judgment'!) The popular expectation of a Messiah once more became prominent; attention was fixed upon one historical moment: the 'Kingdom of God' descends to sit in judgment upon his enemies. But this proves that everything was misunderstood: the 'Kingdom of God' regarded as the last scene of the last act, as a promise! But the Gospel had clearly been the living, the fulfilment, the *reality* of this 'Kingdom of God'. It was precisely a death such as Christ's that was this 'Kingdom of God'. It was only now that all the contempt for the Pharisees and the theologians, and all bitter feelings towards them, were introduced into the character of the Master, – and by this means he himself was converted into a Pharisee and a theologian! On the other hand, the savage veneration of these completely unhinged souls could no longer endure that evangelical right of every man to be the child of God, which Jesus had taught: their revenge consisted in *elevating* Jesus in a manner devoid of all reason, and in separating him from themselves: just as, formerly, the Jews, with the view of revenging themselves on their enemies, separated themselves from their God, and placed him high above them. The Only God, and the Only Son of God: – both were products of resentment.

41

– And from this time forward an absurd problem rose into prominence: 'how *could* God allow it to happen?' To this question the disordered minds of the small community found a reply which in its absurdity was literally terrifying: God gave his Son as a *sacrifice* for the forgiveness of sins. Alas! how prompt and sudden was the end of the gospel! Expiatory sacrifice for guilt, and indeed in its most repulsive and barbaric form, – the sacrifice of the *innocent* for the sins of the guilty! What appalling Paganism! – For Jesus himself had done away with the concept 'guilt', – he denied any gulf between God and man, he *lived* this unity between God and man, it was this that constituted *his* 'glad tidings'…. And he did *not* teach it as a privilege! – Thenceforward there was gradually imported into the type of the Saviour the doctrine of the Last Judgment, and of the 'second coming', the doctrine of sacrificial death, and the doctrine of *Resurrection*, by means of which the whole concept 'blessedness', the entire and only reality of the gospel, is conjured away – in favour of a state *after* death!… St Paul, with that rabbinic impudence which characterises all his doings, rationalised this conception, this prostitution of a conception, as follows: 'if Christ did not rise from the dead, our faith is vain'. – And, in a trice, the most contemptible of all unrealisable promises, the *impudent* doctrine of personal immortality, was woven out of the gospel…. St Paul even preached this immortality as a reward.

42

You now realise what it was that came to an end with the death on the cross: a new and thoroughly original effort towards a Buddhistic movement of peace, towards real and *not* merely promised *happiness on earth*. For, as I have already pointed out, this remains the fundamental difference between the two religions of *decadence*: Buddhism promises little but fulfils more, Christianity promises everything but fulfils nothing. – The 'glad tidings' were followed closely by the absolutely *worst* tidings – those of St Paul. Paul is the incarnation of a type which is the reverse of that of the Saviour; he is the genius in hatred, in the standpoint of hatred, and in the relentless logic of hatred. And alas what did this dysangelist not sacrifice to his hatred! Above all the Saviour himself: he nailed him to *his* cross. Christ's life, his example, his doctrine and death, the sense and the right of the gospel – not a vestige of all this was left, once this forger, prompted by his hatred, had understood in it only that which could serve his purpose. *Not* reality: *not* historical truth!... And once more, the sacerdotal instinct of the Jew, perpetrated the same great crime against history, – he simply cancelled the yesterday, and the day before that, out of Christianity; he *contrived of his own accord a history of the birth of Christianity*. He did more: he once more falsified the history of Israel, so as to make it appear as a prologue to *his* mission: all the prophets had referred to *his* 'Saviour'.... Later on the Church even distorted the history of mankind so as to convert it into a prelude to Christianity.... The type of the Saviour, his teaching, his life, his death, the meaning of his death, even the sequel to his death – nothing remained untouched, nothing was left which even remotely resembled reality. St Paul simply transferred the centre of gravity of the whole of that great life, to a place *behind* this life, – in the *lie* of the 'resuscitated' Christ. At bottom, he had no possible use for the life of the Saviour, – he needed the death on the cross, *and* something more. To regard as honest a man like St Paul (a man whose home was the very headquarters of Stoical enlightenment) when he devises a proof of the continued existence of the Saviour out of a hallucination; or even to believe him when he declares that he had this hallucination, would amount to foolishness on the part of a psychologist: St Paul desired the end, consequently he also desired the means.... Even what he himself did not believe, was believed in by the idiots among whom he spread his doctrine. – What he wanted was power; with St Paul the priest again aspired to power, – he could make use only of concepts, doctrines, symbols with which masses may be tyrannised over, and with which herds are formed. What was the only part of Christianity which was subsequently borrowed by Muhamed? St Paul's invention, his expedient for priestly tyranny and to the formation of herds: the belief in immortality – *that is to say, the doctrine of the 'Last Judgment'*....

43

When the centre of gravity of life is laid, *not* in life, but in a beyond – *in nonentity* – life is utterly robbed of its balance. The great lie of personal immortality destroys all reason, all nature in the instincts, – everything in the instincts that is beneficent, that promotes life and that is a guarantee of the future, henceforward aroused suspicion. The very meaning of life is now construed as the effort to live in such a way that life no longer has any point.... Why show any public spirit? Why be grateful for one's origin and one's forebears? Why collaborate with one's fellows, and be confident? Why be concerned about the general weal or strive after it?... All these things are merely so many 'temptations', so many deviations from the 'straight path'. 'One thing only is necessary'.... That everybody, as an 'immortal soul', should have equal rank, that in the totality of beings, the 'salvation' of each individual may lay claim to eternal importance, that insignificant bigots and three-quarter-lunatics may have the right to suppose that the laws of nature may be persistently *broken* on their account, – any such magnification of every kind of selfishness to infinity, to insolence, cannot be branded with sufficient contempt. And yet it is to this miserable flattery of personal vanity that Christianity owes its *triumph*, – by this means it lured all the bungled and the botched, all revolting and revolted people, all abortions, the whole of the refuse and offal of humanity, over to its side. The 'salvation of the soul' – in plain English: 'the world revolves around me'... The poison of the doctrine '*equal* rights for all' – has been dispensed with the greatest thoroughness by Christianity: Christianity, prompted by the most secret recesses of bad instincts, has waged a deadly war upon all feeling of reverence and distance between man and man – that is to say, the *prerequisite* of all elevation, of every growth in culture; out of the resentment of the masses it wrought its *principal weapons* against us, against everything noble, joyful, exalted on earth, against our happiness on earth.... To grant 'immortality' to every St Peter and St Paul, was the greatest, the most vicious outrage upon *noble* humanity that has ever been perpetrated. – And do not let us underestimate the fatal influence which, springing from Christianity, has insinuated itself even into politics! Nowadays no one has the courage of special rights, of rights of dominion, of a feeling of self-respect and of respect for his equals, – of *pathos of distance*. Our politics are diseased with this lack of courage! – The aristocratic attitude of mind has been most thoroughly undermined by the lie of the equality of souls; and if the belief in the 'privilege of the greatest number' creates and will continue to *create revolutions*, – it is Christianity, let there be no doubt about it, and Christian values, which convert every revolution into blood and crime! Christianity is the revolt of all things that crawl on their bellies against everything that is lofty: the gospel of the 'lowly' *lowers*....

44

The Gospels are invaluable as a testimony of the corruption which was already persistent *within* the first Christian communities. That which St Paul, with the logician's cynicism of a Rabbi, carried to its logical conclusion, was nevertheless merely the process of decay which began with the death of the Saviour. – These gospels cannot be read too cautiously; difficulties lurk behind every word they contain. I confess, and people will not take this amiss, that they are precisely on that account a joy of the first rank for a psychologist, – as the reverse of all naive perversity, as refinement *par excellence*, as a masterpiece of art in psychological corruption. The gospels stand alone. Altogether the Bible allows of no comparison. The *first* thing to be remembered if we do not wish to lose the scent here, is, that we are among Jews. The dissembling of holiness which, here, literally amounts to genius, and which has never been even approximately achieved elsewhere either by books or by men, this fraud in word and pose which in this book is elevated to an *Art*, is not the accident of any individual gift, of any exceptional nature. These qualities are a matter of *race*. With Christianity, the art of telling holy lies, which constitutes the whole of Judaism, reaches its final mastership, thanks to many centuries of Jewish and most thoroughly serious training and practice. The Christian, this *ultima ratio* of falsehood, is the Jew over again – he is even three times a Jew.... The fundamental will only to make use of concepts, symbols and poses, which are demonstrated by the practice of the priests, the instinctive repudiation of every other kind of practice, every other standpoint of valuation and of utility – all this is not only tradition, it is *hereditary*; only as an inheritance is it able to work like nature. The whole of mankind, the best brains, and even the best ages – (one man only excepted who is perhaps only a monster) – have allowed themselves to be deceived. The gospels were read as the *book of innocence*... this is no insignificant sign of the virtuosity with which deception has been practised here. – Of course, if we could only succeed in seeing all these amazing bigots and pretended saints, even for a moment, all would be at an end – and it is precisely because I can read no single word of theirs, without seeing their pretentious poses, *that I have made an end of them*.... I cannot endure a certain way they have of casting their eyes heavenwards. – Fortunately for Christianity, books are for the greatest number, merely *literature*. We must not let ourselves be led away: 'judge not!' they say, but they dispatch all those to hell who stand in their way. Inasmuch as they let God do the judging, they themselves, judge; inasmuch as they glorify God, they glorify themselves; inasmuch as they *exact* those virtues of which they themselves happen to be capable – nay more, of which they are in need in order to be able to remain on top at all; – they assume the grand airs of struggling for virtue, of struggling for the dominion of virtue. 'We live, we die, we sacrifice ourselves for the good' ('the Truth', 'the Light', 'the Kingdom of God'): as a matter of fact they do only what they cannot help doing. Like sneaks they have to play a humble part; sit away in corners, and remain obscurely in the shade, and they make all this appear a duty; their humble life now appears as a *duty*, and their humility is one proof the more of their piety!... Oh, what a humble, chaste and compassionate kind of falsity! 'Virtue itself shall bear us testimony'.... Only read the gospels as books calculated to seduce by means of morality: morality is appropriated by these petty people, – they know what morality can do! The best way of leading mankind by the nose is with morality! The fact is that the most conscious *conceit* of people who believe themselves to be *chosen*, here simulates modesty: in this way they, the Christian community, the 'good and the just' place themselves once and for all on a certain side, the side 'of Truth' – and the rest of mankind, 'the world' on the other.... This was the most fatal kind of megalomania that had ever yet existed on earth: insignificant little abortions of bigots and liars began to lay sole claim to the concepts 'God', 'Truth', 'Light', 'Spirit', 'Love', 'Wisdom', 'Life', as if these things were, so to speak, synonyms of themselves, in order to fence themselves off from 'the world'; little ultra-Jews, ripe for every kind of madhouse, twisted values round in order to suit themselves, just as if the Christian, alone, were the meaning, the salt, the standard and even the '*ultimate tribunal*' of all the rest of mankind.... The whole fatality was rendered possible only because a kind of megalomania, akin to this one and allied to it in race, – the Jewish kind – was already to hand in the world: the very moment the gulf between Jews and Judæo-Christians was opened, the latter had no alternative left, but to adopt the same self-preservative measures as the Jewish instinct suggested, even *against* the Jews themselves, whereas the Jews, theretofore, had employed these same measures only against the Gentiles. The Christian is nothing more than an anarchical Jew.

45

Let me give you a few examples of what these paltry people have stuffed into their heads, what they have laid *on the lips of their Master*: quite a host of confessions from 'beautiful souls'. –

'And whosoever shall not receive you, nor hear you, when ye depart thence, shake off the dust under your feet for a testimony against them. Verily I say unto you, It shall be more tolerable for Sodom and Gomorrah in the day of judgment, than for that city.' (Mark vi. 11.) – *How evangelical!*...

'And whosoever shall offend one of these little ones that believe in me, it is better for him that a millstone were hanged about his neck, and he were cast into the sea.' (Mark ix. 42.) – How *evangelical!*...

'And if thine eye offend thee, pluck it out: it is better for thee to enter into the kingdom of God with one eye, than having two eyes to be cast into hell fire: where their worm dieth not, and the fire is not quenched.' (Mark ix. 47, 48.) – The eye is not precisely what is meant in this passage....

'Verily I say unto you, That there be some of them that stand here, which shall not taste of death, till they have seen the kingdom of God come with power.' (Mark ix. 1.) – Well *lied*, lion!*...

'Whosoever will come after me, let him deny himself, and take up his cross, and follow me. For...' (*A psychologist's comment*. Christian morality is refuted by its 'For's': its "reasons" refute, – this is Christian.) (Mark viii. 34.)

'Judge not, that ye be not judged. For with what judgment ye judge,

---

* An adaptation of Shakespeare's 'Well roared, lion' (*Mid. N. D.*, Act 5, Sc. i.), the lion, as is well known, being the symbol for St Mark in Christian literature and art – TR.

ye shall be judged.' (Matthew vii. I, 2.) – What a strange notion of justice on the part of a 'just' judge!...

'For if ye love them which love you, what reward have ye? do not even the publicans the same? And if ye salute your brethren only, what do ye more *than others*? do not even the publicans so?' (Matthew v. 46, 47.) The principle of 'Christian love': it insists upon being *well paid*....

'But if ye forgive not men their trespasses neither will your Father forgive your trespasses.' (Matthew vi. 15.) – Very compromising for the 'Father' in question.

'But seek ye first the kingdom of God, and his righteousness; and all these things shall be added unto you.' (Matthew vi. 33) – 'All these things' – that is to say, food, clothing, all the necessities of life. To use a moderate expression, this is an *error*.... Shortly before this God appears as a tailor, at least in certain cases....

'Rejoice ye in that day, and leap for joy: for, behold, your reward *is* great in heaven: for in the like manner did their fathers unto the prophets.' (Luke vi. 23.) – *Impudent* rabble! They dare to compare themselves with the prophets....

'Know ye not that ye are the temple of God and *that* the Spirit of God dwelleth in you? If any man defile the temple of God, *him shall God destroy*; for the temple of God is holy, which *temple ye are.*' (St Paul, I Corinthians iii. 16, 17.) – One cannot have too much contempt for this sort of thing....

'Do ye not know that the saints shall judge the world? and if the world shall be judged by you, are ye unworthy to judge the smallest matters?' (St Paul, I Corinthians vi. 2.) – Unfortunately this is not merely the speech of a lunatic.... This *appalling impostor* proceeds thus: 'Know ye not that we shall judge angels? how much more things that pertain to this life?'

'Hath not God made foolish the wisdom of this world? For after that in the wisdom of God, the world by wisdom knew not God, it pleased God by the foolishness of preaching to save them that believe... not many wise men after the flesh, not many mighty, not many noble *are called*; But God hath chosen the foolish things of the world to confound the wise; and God hath chosen the weak things of the world to confound the things which are mighty; And base things of the world, and things which are despised, hath God chosen; *yea*, and things which are not, to bring to nought things that are:

That no flesh should glory in his presence.' (St Paul, I Corinthians i. 20 *et seq.*) – In order to *understand* this passage, which is of the highest importance as an example of the psychology of every Chandala morality, the reader should refer to my *Genealogy of Morals*: in this book, the contrast between a *noble* and a Chandala morality born of *resentment* and impotent revengefulness, is brought to light for the first time. St Paul was the greatest of all the apostles of revenge....

46

What follows from this? That one does well to put on one's gloves when reading the New Testament. The proximity of so much pitch almost defiles one. We should feel just as little inclined to hobnob with 'the first Christians' as with Polish Jews: not that we need explain our objections.... They simply smell bad. – In vain have I sought for a single sympathetic feature in the New Testament; there is not a trace of freedom, kindliness, open-heartedness and honesty to be found in it. Humaneness has not even made a start in this book, while *cleanly* instincts are entirely absent from it.... Only evil instincts are to be found in the New Testament, it shows no sign of courage, these people lßack even the courage of their evil instincts. All is cowardice, all is a closing of one's eyes and self-deception. Every book becomes clean, after one has just read the New Testament: for instance, immediately after laying down St Paul, I read with particular delight that most charming and most wanton of scoffers, Petronius, of whom someone might say what Domenico Boccaccio wrote to the Duke of Parma about Cæsar Borgia: '*è tutto festo*' – immortally healthy, immortally cheerful and well-constituted.... These petty bigots err in their calculations and in the most important thing of all. They certainly attack; but everything they assail is, by that very fact alone, *distinguished*. He whom a 'primitive Christian' attacks, is *not* thereby sullied.... Conversely it is an honour to be opposed by 'primitive Christians'. One cannot read the New Testament without feeling a preference for everything in it which is the subject of abuse – not to speak of the 'wisdom of this world', which an impudent windbag tries in vain to confound 'by the foolishness of preaching'. Even the Pharisees and the Scribes derive advantage from such opposition: they must certainly have been worth something in order to have been hated in such a disreputable way. Hypocrisy – as if this were a reproach which the 'first Christians' *were at liberty to make!* – After all the Scribes and Pharisees were the *privileged ones*; this was quite enough, the hatred of the Chandala requires no other reasons. I very much fear that the 'first Christian' – as also the '*last Christian*' *whom I may yet be able to meet,* – is in his deepest instincts a rebel against everything privileged; he lives and struggles unremittingly for 'equal rights'!... Regarded more closely, he has no alternative.... If one's desire be personally to represent 'one of the chosen of God' – or a 'temple of God', or 'a judge of angels', – then every other principle of selection, for instance that based upon a standard of honesty, intellect, manliness and pride, or upon beauty and freedom of heart, becomes the 'world', – *evil in itself.* Moral: every word on the lips of a 'first Christian' is a lie, every action he does is an instinctive falsehood, – all his values, all his aims are pernicious; but the man he, hates, *the thing* he hates, *has value*.... The Christian, more particularly the Christian priest, is a *criterion of values* – Do I require to add that in the whole of the New Testament only one figure appears which we cannot help respecting? Pilate, the Roman Governor. To take a Jewish quarrel *seriously* was a thing he could not get himself to do. One Jew more or less – what did it matter?... The noble scorn of a Roman, in whose presence the word 'truth' had been shamelessly abused, has enriched the New Testament with the only saying which *is of value*, – and this saying is not only the criticism, but actually the shattering of that Testament: 'What is truth!'...

47

That which separates us from other people is not the fact that we can discover no God, either in history, or in nature, or behind nature, – but that we regard what has been revered as 'God', not as 'divine', but as wretched, absurd, pernicious; not as an error, but as a *crime against life*.... We deny God as God.... If the existence of this Christian God were *proved* to us, we should feel even less able to believe in him. – In a formula: *deus qualem Paulus creavit, dei negatio.* – A religion such as Christianity which never once comes in touch with reality, and which collapses the very moment reality asserts its rights even on one single point, must naturally be a mortal enemy of the 'wisdom of this world' – that is to say, *science*. It will call all those means good with which mental discipline, lucidity and severity in intellectual matters, nobility and freedom of the intellect may be poisoned, calumniated and *decried*. 'Faith' as an imperative is a *veto* against science, – in praxi, it means lies at any price. St Paul *understood* that falsehood – that 'faith' was necessary; subsequently the Church understood St Paul. – That 'God' which St Paul invented for himself, a God who 'confounds' the 'wisdom of this world' (in a narrower sense, the two great opponents of all superstition, philology and medicine), means, in very truth, simply St Paul's firm *resolve* to do so: to call his own will 'God,' *thora*, that is arch-Jewish. St Paul insists upon confounding the 'wisdom of this world': his enemies are the *good old* philologists and doctors of the Alexandrine schools; it is on them that he wages war. As a matter of fact no one is either a philologist or a doctor, who is not also an *Antichrist*. As a philologist, for instance, a man sees *behind* the 'holy books', as a doctor he sees *behind* the physiological rottenness of the typical Christian. The doctor says 'incurable', the philologist says 'forgery'.

48

Has anybody ever really understood the celebrated story which stands at the beginning of the Bible, – concerning God's deadly panic over *science*?... Nobody has understood it. This essentially sacerdotal book naturally begins with the great inner difficulty of the priest: *he* knows only one great danger, *consequently* 'God' has only one great danger. –

The old God, entirely 'spirit', a high-priest through and through, and wholly perfect, is wandering in a leisurely fashion round his garden; but he is bored. Against boredom even the gods themselves struggle in vain.* What does he do? He invents man, – man is entertaining.... But, behold, even man begins to be bored. God's compassion for the only form of misery which is peculiar to all paradises, exceeds all bounds: so forthwith he creates yet other animals. God's *first* mistake: man did not think animals entertaining, – he dominated them, he did not even wish to be an 'animal'. Consequently God created woman. And boredom did indeed cease from that moment, – but many other

---

* A parody on a line in Schiller's '*Jungfrau von Orleans*' (Act 3, Sc. vi.): '*Mit der Dummheit kämpfen Götter selbst vergebens.*' (With stupidity even the gods themselves struggle in vain). – TR.

things ceased as well! Woman was God's *second* mistake. – 'Woman in her innermost nature is a serpent, Heva' – every priest knows this: 'all evil came into this world through woman,' – every priest knows this too. '*Consequently science* also comes from woman'…. Only through woman did man learn to taste of the tree of knowledge. – What had happened? Panic had seized the old God. Man himself had been his *greatest* mistake, he had created a rival for himself, science makes you *equal to God*, – it is all up with priests and gods when man becomes scientific! – Moral: science is the most prohibited thing of all, – it alone, is forbidden. Science is the *first*, the germ of all sins, the original sin. *This alone is morality*. – 'Thou shalt *not* know': – the rest follows as a matter of course, God's panic did not deprive him of his intelligence. How can one *guard* against science? For ages this was his principal problem. Reply: man must be kicked out of paradise! Happiness, leisure leads to thinking, – all thoughts are bad thoughts…. Man *must* not think. – And the 'priest-per-se' proceeds to invent distress, death, the vital danger of pregnancy, every kind of misery, decrepitude, and affliction, and above all *disease*, – all these are but weapons employed in the struggle with science! Trouble prevents man from thinking…. And notwithstanding all these precautions! Oh, horror! the work of science towers aloft, it storms heaven itself, it rings the death-knell of the gods, – what's to be done? – The old God invents *war*; he separates the nations, and contrives to make men destroy each other mutually (the priests have always been in need of war…). War, among other things, is a great disturber of science! – Incredible! Knowledge, *the rejection of the sacerdotal yoke*, nevertheless increases. – So the old God arrives at this final decision: 'Man has become scientific, – *there is no help for it, he must be drowned!*'…

49

You have understood me. The beginning of the Bible contains the whole psychology of the priest – The priest knows only one great danger, and that is science, – the healthy concept of cause and effect. But, on the whole, science flourishes only under happy conditions, – a man must have time, he must also have superfluous mental energy in order to 'pursue knowledge'… '*Consequently* man must be made unhappy,' – this has been the argument of the priest of all ages. – You have already divined what, in accordance with such a manner of arguing, must first have come into the world: – 'sin'…. The notion of guilt and punishment, the whole 'moral order of the universe', was invented against science, – against the deliverance of man from the priest…. Man must *not* cast his glance upon the outer world, he must turn it inwards into himself; he must not as a learner look cleverly and cautiously *into* things; he must not see at all: he must suffer…. And he must *suffer*, so that he may be in need of the priest every minute. – Away with doctors! What is needed is a Saviour! – The notion of guilt and punishment, including the doctrine of 'grace', of 'salvation' and of 'forgiveness' – all *lies* through and through without a shred of psychological reality – were invented in order to destroy man's *sense of causality*: they are an attack on the concept of cause and effect! – And *not* an attack with the fist, with the knife, with honesty in hate and love! But one actuated by the most cowardly, most crafty, and most ignoble instincts! A *priest's* attack! A *parasite's* attack! A vampyrism of pale subterranean leeches! – … When the natural consequences of an act are no longer 'natural', but are thought to be conjured up by phantom concepts of superstition, by 'God', by 'spirits', and by 'souls', as merely moral consequences, in the form of rewards, punishments, hints, and educational means, – then the whole basis of knowledge is destroyed, – *then the greatest crime against man has been perpetrated.* – Sin, I repeat, this form of self-pollution *par excellence* on the part of man, was invented in order to make science, culture and every elevation and noble trait in man quite impossible; by means of the invention of sin the priest is able to *rule*.

50

I cannot here dispense with a psychology of 'faith' and of the 'faithful', which will naturally be to the advantage of the 'faithful'. If today there are still many who do not know how very *indecent* it is to be a 'believer' – or to what extent such a state is the sign of decadence, and of the broken will to life, – they will know it no later than tomorrow. My voice can make even those hear who are hard of hearing. – If perchance my ears have not deceived me, it seems that among Christians there is such a thing as a kind of criterion of truth, which is called 'the proof of power'. 'Faith saveth; *therefore* it is true.' – It might be objected here that it is precisely salvation which is not proved but only *promised*: salvation is bound up with the condition 'faith', – one *shall* be saved, *because* one has faith…. But how prove *that* that which the priest promises to the faithful really will take place, to wit: the 'Beyond' which defies all demonstration? – The assumed 'proof of power' is at bottom once again only a belief in the fact that the effect which faith promises will not fail to take place. In a formula: 'I believe that faith saveth; – consequently it is true.' – But with this we are at the end of our tether. This *'consequently'* would be the *absurdum* itself as a criterion of truth. – Let us be indulgent enough to assume, however, that salvation is proved by faith (*not* only desired, and *not* merely promised by the somewhat suspicious lips of a priest): could salvation – or, in technical terminology, *happiness* – ever be a proof of truth? So little is it so that, when pleasurable sensations make their influence felt in replying to the question 'what is true', they furnish almost the contradiction of truth, or at any rate they make it in the highest degree suspicious. The proof through 'happiness', is a proof of happiness – and nothing else; why in the world should we take it for granted that *true* judgments cause more pleasure than false ones, and that in accordance with a pre-established harmony, they necessarily bring pleasant feelings in their wake? – The experience of all strict and profound minds teaches the *reverse*. Every inch of truth has been conquered only after a struggle, almost everything to which our heart, our love and our trust in life cleaves, has had to be sacrificed for it. Greatness of soul is necessary for this: the service of truth is the hardest of all services. – What then is meant by honesty in things intellectual? It means that a man is severe towards his own heart, that he scorns 'beautiful feelings', and that he makes a matter of conscience out of every yea and nay! – Faith saveth: *consequently* it lies….

51

The fact that faith may in certain circumstances save, the fact that salvation as the result of an *idée fixe* does not constitute a true idea, the fact that faith moves *no* mountains, but may very readily raise them where previously they did not exist – all these things are made sufficiently clear by a mere casual stroll through a *lunatic asylum*. Of course *no* priest would find this sufficient: for he instinctively denies that illness is illness or that lunatic asylums are lunatic asylums.

Christianity is in *need* of illness, just as Ancient Greece was in need of a superabundance of health. The actual ulterior motive of the whole of the Church's system of salvation is to *make people ill*. And is not the Church itself the Catholic madhouse as an ultimate ideal? – The earth as a whole converted into a madhouse? – The kind of religious man which the Church aims at producing is a typical *decadent*. The moment of time at which a religious crisis attains the ascendancy over a people, is always characterised by nerve-epidemics; the 'inner world' of the religious man is ridiculously like the 'inner world' of over-irritable and exhausted people; the 'highest' states which Christianity holds up to mankind as the value of values, are epileptic in character, – the Church has pronounced only madmen or great swindlers *in majorem dei honorem* holy. Once I ventured to characterise the whole of the Christian training of penance and salvation (which nowadays is best studied in England) as a *folie circulaire* methodically generated upon a soil which, of course, is already prepared for it, – that is to say, which is thoroughly morbid. Not everyone who likes can be a Christian: no man is 'converted' to Christianity, – he must be sick enough for it... We others who possess enough courage both for health and for contempt, how rightly *we* may despise a religion which taught men to misunderstand the body! which would not rid itself of the superstitions of the soul! which made a virtue of taking inadequate nourishment! which in health combats a sort of enemy, devil, temptation! which persuaded itself that it was possible to bear a perfect soul about in a cadaverous body, and which, to this end, had to make up for itself a new concept of 'perfection', a pale, sickly, idiotically gushing ideal, – so-called 'holiness', – holiness, which in itself is simply a symptom of an impoverished, enervated and incurably deteriorated body!... The movement of Christianity, as a European movement, was from first to last, a general accumulation of the ruck and scum of all sorts and kinds (and these, by means of Christianity, aspire to power). It does not express the downfall of a race, it is rather a conglomerate assembly of all the decadent elements from everywhere which seek each other and crowd together. It was not, as some believe, the corruption of antiquity, of *noble* antiquity, which made Christianity possible: the learned idiocy which nowadays tries to support such a notion cannot be too severely contradicted. At the time when the morbid and corrupted Chandala classes became Christianised in the whole of the *imperium*, the very *contrary type*, nobility, was extant in its finest and maturest forms. The greatest number became master; the democracy of Christian instincts triumphed.... Christianity was not 'national', it was not determined by race, – it appealed to all the disinherited forms of life, it had its allies everywhere. Christianity is built upon the rancour of the sick; its instinct is directed *against* the sound, against health. Everything well-constituted, proud, high-spirited, and beautiful is offensive to its ears and eyes. Again I remind you of St Paul's priceless words: 'And God hath chosen the *weak* things of the world, the *foolish* things of the world; and *base* things of the world, and things which are *despised*': this was the formula, *in hoc signo* decadence triumphed. – *God on the Cross* – does no one yet understand the terrible ulterior motive of this symbol? – Everything that suffers, everything that hangs on the cross, is *divine*.... All of us hang on the cross, consequently we are *divine*.... We alone are divine.... Christianity was a victory; a *nobler* type of character perished through it, – Christianity has been humanity's greatest misfortune hitherto. –

52

Christianity also stands opposed to everything happily constituted in the *mind*, – it can make use only of morbid reason as Christian reason; it takes the side of everything idiotic, it utters a curse upon 'intellect', upon the *superbia* of the healthy intellect. Since illness belongs to the essence of Christianity, the typically Christian state, 'faith', *must* also be a form of illness, and all straight, honest and scientific roads to knowledge must be repudiated by the Church as forbidden.... Doubt in itself is already a sin.... The total lack of psychological cleanliness in the priest, which reveals itself in his look, is a *result* of decadence. Hysterical women, as also children with scrofulous constitutions, should be observed as a proof of how invariably instinctive falsity, the love of lying for the sake of lying, and the inability either to look or to walk straight, are the expression of decadence. 'Faith' simply means the refusal to know what is true. The pious person, the priest of both sexes, is false because he is ill: his instinct *demands* that truth should not assert its right anywhere. 'That which makes ill is good: that which proceeds from abundance, from superabundance and from power, is evil': that is the view of the faithful. The *constraint to lie* – that is the sign by which I recognise every predetermined theologian. – Another characteristic of the theologian is his lack of *capacity for philology*. What I mean here by the word philology is, in a general sense to be understood as the art of reading well, of being able to take account of facts *without* falsifying them by interpretation, without losing either caution, patience or subtlety owing to one's desire to understand. Philology as *ephexis** in interpretation, whether one be dealing with books, newspaper reports, human destinies or meteorological records, – not to speak of the 'salvation of the soul'.... The manner in which a theologian, whether in Berlin or in Rome, interprets a verse from the 'Scriptures', or an experience, or the triumph of his nation's army for instance, under the superior guiding light of David's Psalms, is always so exceedingly *daring*, that it is enough to make a philologist's hair stand on end. And what is he to do, when pietists and other cows from Swabia explain their miserable everyday lives in their smoky hovels by means of the 'Finger of God', a miracle of 'grace', of 'Providence', of experiences of 'salvation'! The most modest effort of the intellect, not to speak of decent feeling, ought at least to lead these interpreters to convince themselves of the absolute childishness and unworthiness of any such abuse of the dexterity of God's fingers. However small an amount of loving piety we might possess, a god who cured us in time of a cold in the nose, or who arranged for us to enter a carriage just at the moment when a cloud burst over our heads, would be such an absurd God, that he would have to be abolished, even if he existed.** God as a domestic servant, as a postman, as a general provider, – in short, merely a word for the most foolish kind of accidents.... 'Divine Providence', as it is believed in today by almost every third man in 'cultured Germany', would be

---

* ἔφεξις = Lat. *retentio, inhibitio* (Stephanus, *Thesaurus Græcæ Linguæ*); therefore: reserve, caution. The Greek Sceptics were also called Ephectics owing to their caution in judging and in concluding from facts. – TR.

** The following passage from Multatuti will throw light on this passage: – 'Father: – "Behold, my son, how wisely Providence has arranged everything! This bird lays its eggs in its nest and the young will be hatched just about the time when there will be worms and flies with which to feed them. Then they will sing a song of praise in honour of the Creator who overwhelms his creatures with blessings." – "Son: – 'Will the worms join in the song, Dad?'". – TR.

an argument against God, in fact it would be the strongest argument against God that could be imagined. And in any case it is an argument against the Germans.

53

The notion that martyrs prove anything at all in favour of a thing, is so exceedingly doubtful, that I would fain deny that there has ever yet existed a martyr who had anything to do with truth. In the very manner in which a martyr flings his little parcel of truth at the head of the world, such a low degree of intellectual honesty and such obtuseness in regard to the question 'truth' makes itself felt, that one never requires to refute a martyr. Truth is not a thing which one might have and another be without: only peasants or peasant-apostles, after the style of Luther, can think like this about truth. You may be quite sure, that the greater a man's degree of conscientiousness may be in matters intellectual, the more modest he will show himself on this point. To *know* about five things, and with a subtle wave of the hand to refuse to know *others*.... 'Truth' as it is understood by every prophet, every sectarian, every free thinker, every socialist and every churchman, is an absolute proof of the fact that these people haven't even begun that discipline of the mind and that process of self-mastery, which is necessary for the discovery of any small, even exceedingly small truth. – Incidentally, the deaths of martyrs have been a great misfortune in the history of the world: they led people astray.... The conclusion which all idiots, women and common people come to, that there must be something in a cause for which someone lays down his life (or which, as in the case of primitive Christianity, provokes an epidemic of sacrifices), – this conclusion put a tremendous check upon all investigation, upon the spirit of investigation and of caution. Martyrs have *harmed* the cause of truth.... Even to this day it only requires the crude fact of persecution, in order to create an honourable name for any obscure sect who does not matter in the least. What? is a cause actually changed in any way by the fact that someone has laid down his life for it? An error which becomes honourable, is simply an error that possesses one seductive charm the more: do you suppose, dear theologians, that we shall give you the chance of acting the martyrs for your lies? – A thing is refuted by being laid respectfully on ice, and theologians are refuted in the same way. This was precisely the world-historic foolishness of all persecutors; they lent the thing they combated a semblance of honour by conferring the fascination of martyrdom upon it.... Women still lie prostrate before an error today, because they have been told that someone died on the cross for it. *Is the cross then an argument?* – But concerning all these things, one person alone has said what mankind has been in need of for thousands of years, – *Zarathustra*.

'Letters of blood did they write on the way they went, and their folly taught that truth is proved by blood.

'But blood is the very worst testimony of truth; blood poisoneth even the purest teaching, and turneth it into delusion and into blood feuds.

'And when a man goeth through fire for his teaching – what does that prove? Verily, it is more when out of one's own burning springeth one's own teaching.'*

54

Do not allow yourselves to be deceived: great minds are sceptical. Zarathustra is a sceptic. Strength and the *freedom* which proceeds from the power and excessive power of the mind, *manifests* itself through scepticism. Men of conviction are of no account whatever in regard to any principles of value or of non-value. Convictions are prisons. They never see far enough, they do not look down from a sufficient height: but in order to have any say in questions of value and non-value, a man must see five hundred convictions *beneath* him, – *behind* him.... A spirit who desires great things, and who also desires the means thereto, is necessarily a sceptic. Freedom from every kind of conviction *belongs* to strength, to the *ability* to open one's eyes freely.... The great passion of a sceptic, the basis and power of his being, which is more enlightened and more despotic than he is himself, enlists all his intellect into its service; it makes him unscrupulous; it even gives him the courage to employ unholy means; in certain circumstances it even allows him convictions. Conviction as a *means*: much is achieved merely by means of a conviction. Great passion makes use of and consumes convictions, it does not submit to them – it knows that it is a sovereign power. Conversely; the need of faith, of anything either absolutely affirmative or negative, Carlylism (if I may be allowed this expression), is the need of weakness. The man of beliefs, the 'believer'

---

*   *Thus Spake Zarathustra*. The Priests. – TR.

of every sort and condition, is necessarily a dependent man; – he is one who cannot regard *himself* as an aim, who cannot postulate aims from the promptings of his own heart The 'believer' does not belong to himself, he can be only a means, he must be *used up*, he is in need of someone who uses him up. His instinct accords the highest honour to a morality of self-abnegation: everything in him, his prudence, his experience, his vanity, persuade him to adopt this morality. Every sort of belief is in itself an expression of self-denial, of self-estrangement....
If one considers how necessary a regulating code of conduct is to the majority of people, a code of conduct which constrains them and fixes them from outside; and how control, or in a higher sense, *slavery*, is the only and ultimate condition under which the weak-willed man, and especially woman, flourish; one also understands conviction, 'faith'. The man of conviction finds in the latter his *backbone*. To be *blind* to many things, to be impartial about nothing, to belong always to a particular side, to hold a strict and necessary point of view in all matters of values – these are the only conditions under which such a man can survive at all. But all this is the reverse of, the antagonist of, the truthful man, – of truth.... The believer is not at liberty to have a conscience for the question 'true' and 'untrue': to be upright on *this* point would mean his immediate downfall. The pathological limitations of his standpoint convert the convinced man into the fanatic – Savonarola, Luther, Rousseau, Robespierre, Saint-Simon, – these are the reverse type of the strong spirit that has become *free*. But the grandiose poses of these *morbid* spirits, of these epileptics of ideas, exercise an influence over the masses, – fanatics are picturesque, mankind prefers to look at poses than to listen to reason.

55

One step further in the psychology of conviction of 'faith'. It is already some time since I first thought of considering whether convictions were not perhaps more dangerous enemies of truth than lies ('Human All-too-Human', Part I, Aphs. 54 and 483). Now I would fain put the decisive question: is there any difference at all between a lie and a conviction? – All the world believes that there is, but what in Heaven's name does not all the world believe! Every conviction has its history, its preliminary stages, its period of groping and of mistakes: it becomes a conviction only after it has not been one for a long time, only after

it has *scarcely* been one for a long time. What? might not falsehood
be the embryonic form of conviction? – At times all that is required
is a change of personality: very often what was a lie in the father
becomes a conviction in the son. – I call a lie, to refuse to see something
that one sees, to refuse to see it exactly *as* one sees it: whether a lie
is perpetrated before witnesses or not is beside the point. – The most
common sort of lie is the one uttered to one's self; to lie to others is
relatively exceptional. Now this refusal to see what one sees, this
refusal to see a thing exactly as one sees it, is almost the first condition
for all those who belong to a *party* in any sense whatsoever: the man
who belongs to a party perforce becomes a liar. German historians,
for instance, are convinced that Rome stood for despotism, whereas
the Teutons introduced the spirit of freedom into the world: what
difference is there between this conviction and a lie? After this is it to
be wondered at, that all parties, including German historians,
instinctively adopt the grandiloquent phraseology of morality, – that
morality almost owes its *survival* to the fact that the man who belongs
to a party, no matter what it may be, is in need of morality every
moment? – 'This is our conviction: we confess it to the whole world,
we live and die for it, – let us respect everything that has a conviction!'
– I have actually heard anti-semites speak in this way. On the contrary,
my dear sirs! An antisemite does not become the least bit more
respectable because he lies on principle…. Priests, who in such matters
are more subtle, and who perfectly understand the objection to which
the idea of a conviction lies open – that is to say of a falsehood which
is perpetrated on principle *because* it serves a purpose, borrowed from
the Jews the prudent measure of setting the concept 'God', 'Will of
God', 'Revelation of God', at this place. Kant, too, with his categorical
imperative, was on the same road: this was his *practical* reason. – There
are some questions in which it is *not* given to man to decide between
true and false; all the principal questions, all the principal problems
of value, stand beyond human reason…. To comprehend the limits of
reason – this alone is genuine philosophy. For what purpose did God
give man revelation? Would God have done anything superfluous? Man
cannot of his own accord know what is good and what is evil, that is
why God taught man his will…. Moral: the priest does *not* lie, such
questions as 'truth' or 'falseness' have nothing to do with the things
concerning which the priest speaks; such things do not allow of lying.

For, in order to lie, it would be necessary to know *what* is true in this respect. But that is precisely what man cannot know: hence the priest is only the mouthpiece of God. – This sort of sacerdotal syllogism is by no means exclusively Judaic or Christian; the right to lie and the *prudent measure* of 'revelation' belongs to the priestly type, whether of decadent periods or of Pagan times (– Pagans are all those who say yea to life, and to whom 'God' is the word for the great yea to all things). The 'law', the 'will of God', the 'holy book', and inspiration. – All these things are merely words for the conditions under which the priest attains to power, and with which he maintains his power, – these concepts are to be found at the base of all sacerdotal organisations, of all priestly or philosophical and ecclesiastical governments. The 'holy lie', which is common to Confucius, to the law-book of Manu, to Muhamed, and to the Christian church, is not even absent in Plato. 'Truth is here'; this phrase means, wherever it is uttered: *the priest lies....*

56

After all, the question is, to what *end* are falsehoods perpetrated? The fact that, in Christianity, 'holy' ends are entirely absent, constitutes *my* objection to the means it employs. Its ends are only *bad* ends: the poisoning, the calumniation and the denial of life, the contempt of the body, the degradation and self-pollution of man by virtue of the concept sin, – consequently its means are bad as well. – My feelings are quite the reverse when I read the law-book of *Manu*, an incomparably superior and more intellectual work, which it would be a sin against the *spirit* even to *mention* in the same breath with the Bible. You will guess immediately why: it has a genuine philosophy behind it, *in* it, not merely an evil-smelling Jewish distillation of Rabbinism and superstition, – it gives something to chew even to the most fastidious psychologist. And, *not* to forget the most important point of all, it is fundamentally different from every kind of Bible: by means of it the *noble classes*, the philosophers and the warriors guard and guide the masses; it is replete with noble values, it is filled with a feeling of perfection, with a saying of yea to life, and a triumphant sense of well-being in regard to itself and to life, – the sun shines upon the whole book. – All those things which Christianity smothers with its bottomless vulgarity: procreation, woman, marriage, are here treated with earnestness, with reverence, with love and confidence. How can one possibly place in the hands of children and women, a book that contains those vile words: 'to avoid fornication, let every man have his own wife, and let every woman have her own husband... it is better to marry than to burn.'* And is it decent to be a Christian so long as the very origin of man is Christianised, – that is to say, befouled, by the idea of the *immaculata conceptio*?... I know of no book in which so many delicate and kindly things are said to woman, as in the Law-Book of Manu; these old grey-beards and saints have a manner of being gallant to women which, perhaps, cannot be surpassed. 'The mouth of a woman,' says Manu on one occasion, 'the breast of a maiden, the prayer of a child, and the smoke of the sacrifice, are always pure.' Elsewhere he says: 'there is nothing purer than the light of the sun, the shadow cast by a cow, air, water, fire and the breath of a maiden.' And finally – perhaps this is also a holy lie: – 'all the openings of the body above the navel are pure, all those below the navel are impure. Only in a maiden is the whole body pure.'

57

The unholiness of Christian means is caught *in flagranti*, if only the end aspired to by Christianity be compared with that of the Law-Book of Manu; if only these two utterly opposed aims be put under a strong light. The critic of Christianity simply cannot avoid making Christianity *contemptible*. – A Law-Book like that of Manu comes into being like every good law-book: it epitomises the experience, the precautionary measures, and the experimental morality of long ages, it settles things definitely, it no longer creates. The prerequisite for a codification of this kind, is the recognition of the fact that the means which procure authority for a *truth* to which it has cost both time and great pains to attain, are fundamentally different from those with which that same truth would be proved. A law-book never relates the utility, the reasons, the preliminary casuistry, of a law: for it would be precisely in this way that it would forfeit its imperative tone, the 'thou shalt', the first condition of its being obeyed. The problem lies exactly in this. – At a certain stage in the development of a people, the most far-seeing class within it (that is to say, the class that sees farthest backwards

---

* I Corinthians vii. 2, 9. – TR.

and forwards), declares the experience of how its fellow-creatures ought to live – *can* live – to be finally settled. Its object is, to reap as rich and as complete a harvest as possible, in return for the ages of experiment and *terrible* experience it has traversed. Consequently, that which has to be avoided, above all, is any further experimentation, the continuation of the state when values are still fluid, the testing, choosing, and criticising of values *in infinitum*. Against all this a double wall is built up: in the first place, *revelation*, which is the assumption that the rationale of every law is not human in its origin, that it was not sought and found after ages of error, but that it is divine in its origin, completely and utterly without a history, gift, a miracle, a mere communication.... And secondly, *tradition*, which is the assumption that the law has obtained since the most primeval times, that it is impious and a crime against one's ancestors to attempt to doubt it. The authority of law is established on the principles: God *gave* it, the ancestors *lived* it. – The superior reason of such a procedure lies in the intention to draw consciousness off step by step from that mode of life which has been recognised as correct (*i.e., proved* after enormous and carefully examined experience), so that perfect automatism of the instincts may be attained, – this being the only possible basis of all mastery of every kind of perfection in the art of life. To draw up a law-book like Manu's, is tantamount to granting a people mastership for the future, perfection for the future, – the right to aspire to the highest art of life. *To that end it must be made unconscious*; this is the object of every holy lie. – *The order of castes*, the highest, the dominating law, is only the sanction of a *natural order*, of a natural legislation of the first rank, over which no arbitrary innovation, no 'modern idea' has any power. Every healthy society falls into three distinct types, which reciprocally condition one another and which gravitate differently in the physiological sense; and each of these has its own hygiene, its own sphere of work, its own special feeling of perfection, and its own mastership. It is nature, not Manu, that separates from the rest, those individuals preponderating in intellectual power, those excelling in muscular strength and temperament, and the third class which is distinguished neither in one way nor the other, the mediocre, – the latter as the greatest number, the former as the *élite*. The superior caste – I call them the fewest, – has, as the perfect caste, the privileges of the *fewest*: it devolves upon them to represent happiness, beauty and goodness on earth. Only the most intellectual men have the right to beauty, to the beautiful: only in them is goodness not weakness. *Pulchrum est paucorum hominum*: goodness is a privilege. On the other hand there is nothing which they should be more strictly forbidden than repulsive manners or a pessimistic look, a look that makes everything *seem ugly*, – or even indignation at the general aspect of things. Indignation is the privilege of the Chandala, and so is pessimism. 'The world is perfect' – that is what the instinct of the most intellectual says, the yea-saying instinct; 'imperfection, every kind of *inferiority* to us, distance, the pathos of distance, even the Chandala belongs to this perfection.' The most intellectual men, as the *strongest* find their happiness where others meet with their ruin: in the labyrinth, in hardness towards themselves and others, in endeavour; their delight is self-mastery: with them asceticism becomes a second nature, a need, an instinct. They regard a difficult task as their privilege; to play with burdens which crush their fellows is to them a *recreation*.... Knowledge, a form of asceticism. – They are the most honourable kind of men: but that does not prevent them from being the most cheerful and most gracious. They rule, not because they will, but because they *are*; they are not at liberty to take a second place. – The second in rank are the guardians of the law, the custodians of order and of security, the noble warriors, the king, above all, as the highest formula of the warrior, the judge, and keeper of the law. The second in rank are the executive of the most intellectual, the nearest to them in duty, relieving them of all that is *coarse* in the work of ruling, – their retinue, their right hand, their best disciples. In all this, I repeat, there is nothing arbitrary, nothing 'artificial', that which is *otherwise* is artificial, – by that which is otherwise, nature is put to shame.... The order of castes, and the order of rank merely formulates the supreme law of life itself; the differentiation of the three types is necessary for the maintenance of society, and for enabling higher and highest types to be reared, – the *inequality* of rights is the only condition of there being rights at all. – A right is a privilege. And in his way, each has his privilege. Let us not underestimate the privileges of the *mediocre*. Life always gets harder towards the summit, – the cold increases, responsibility increases. A high civilisation is a pyramid: it can stand only upon a broad base, its first prerequisite is a strongly and soundly consolidated mediocrity. Handicraft, commerce, agriculture, science, the greater part of art, – in a word, the whole range of professional and business callings, is compatible only with mediocre ability and ambition; such pursuits would be out of place among exceptions, the instinct pertaining thereto would oppose not only aristocracy but anarchy as well. The fact that one is publicly useful, a wheel, a function, presupposes a certain natural destiny: it is not *society*, but the only kind of *happiness* of which the great majority are capable, that makes them intelligent machines. For the mediocre it is a joy to be mediocre; in them mastery in one thing, a speciality, is a natural instinct. It would be absolutely unworthy of a profound thinker to see any objection in mediocrity *per se*. For in itself it is the first essential condition under which exceptions are possible; a high culture is determined by it. When the exceptional man treats the mediocre with more tender care than he does himself or his equals, this is not mere courtesy of heart on his part – but simply his *duty*…. Whom do I hate most among the rabble of the present day? The socialistic rabble, the Chandala apostles, who undermine the working man's instinct, his happiness and his feeling of contentedness with his insignificant existence, – who make him envious, and who teach him revenge…. The wrong never lies in unequal rights; it lies in the claim to equal rights. What is *bad*? But I have already replied to this: Everything that proceeds from weakness, envy and *revenge*. – The anarchist and the Christian are offspring of the same womb….

58

In point of fact, it matters greatly to what end one lies: whether one preserves or *destroys* by means of falsehood. It is quite justifiable to bracket the *Christian* and the *anarchist* together: their object, their instinct, is concerned only with destruction. The proof of this proposition can be read quite plainly from history: history spells it with appalling distinctness. Whereas we have just seen a religious legislation, whose object was to render the highest possible means of making life *flourish*, and of making a grand organisation of society, eternal, – Christianity found its mission in putting an end to such an organisation, *precisely because life flourishes through it*. In the one case, the net profit to the credit of reason, acquired through long ages of experiment and of insecurity, is applied usefully to the most remote ends, and the harvest, which is as large, as rich and as complete as possible, is reaped and garnered: in the other case, on the contrary, the harvest is *blighted* in a single night. That which stood there, *ære perennius*, the *imperium Romanum*, the most magnificent form of organisation, under difficult conditions, that has ever been achieved, and compared with which everything that preceded, and everything which followed it, is mere patchwork, gimcrackery, and dilettantism, – those holy anarchists made it their 'piety', to destroy 'the world' – that is to say, the *imperium Romanum*, until no two stones were left standing one on the other, – until even the Teutons and other clodhoppers were able to become master of it. The Christian and the anarchist are both decadents; they are both incapable of acting in any other way than disintegratingly, poisonously and witheringly, like *bloodsuckers*; they are both actuated by an instinct of *mortal hatred* of everything that stands erect, that is great, that is lasting, and that is a guarantee of the future.... Christianity was the vampire of the *imperium Romanum*, – in a night it shattered the stupendous achievement of the Romans, which was to acquire the territory for a vast civilisation which could bide its time. – Does no one understand this yet? The *imperium Romanum* that we know, and which the history of the Roman province teaches us to know ever more thoroughly, this most admirable work of art on a grand scale, was the beginning, its construction was calculated *to prove* its worth by millenniums, – unto this day nothing has ever again been built in this fashion, nor have men even dreamt since of building on this scale *sub specie aterni*! – This organisation was sufficiently firm to withstand bad emperors: the accident of personalities must have nothing to do with such matters – the first principle of all great architecture. But it was not sufficiently firm to resist the *corruptest* form of corruption, to resist the Christians.... These stealthy canker-worms, which under the shadow of night, mist and duplicity, insinuated themselves into the company of every individual, and proceeded to drain him of all seriousness for real things, of all his instinct for *realities*; this cowardly, effeminate and sugary gang have step by step alienated all 'souls' from this colossal edifice, – those valuable, virile and noble natures who felt that the cause of Rome was their own personal cause, their own personal seriousness, their own personal pride. The stealth of the bigot, the secrecy of the conventicle, concepts as black as hell such as the sacrifice of the innocent, the *unio mystica* in the drinking of blood, above all the slowly kindled fire of revenge, of Chandala revenge – such things became master of Rome, the same kind of religion on the pre-existent form of which Epicurus had waged war. One has only to read Lucretius in order to understand what Epicurus combated, *not* Paganism, but 'Christianity', that is to say the corruption of souls through the concept of guilt, through the concept of punishment and immortality. He combated the *subterranean* cults, the whole of latent Christianity – to deny immortality was at that time a genuine *deliverance*. – And Epicurus had triumphed, every respectable thinker in the Roman Empire was an Epicurean: *then St Paul appeared...* St Paul, the Chandala hatred against Rome, against 'the world', the Jew, the eternal Jew *par excellence,* become flesh and genius.... What he divined was, how, by the help of the small sectarian Christian movement, independent of Judaism, a universal conflagration could be kindled; how, with the symbol of the 'God on the Cross', everything submerged, everything secretly insurrectionary, the whole offspring of anarchical intrigues could be gathered together to constitute an enormous power. 'For salvation is of the Jews.' – Christianity is the formula for the supersession, *and* epitomising of all kinds of subterranean cults, that of Osiris, of the Great Mother, of Mithras for example: St Paul's genius consisted in his discovery of this. In this matter his instinct was so certain, that, regardless of doing violence to truth, he laid the ideas by means of which those Chandala religions fascinated, upon the very lips of the 'Saviour' he had invented, and not only upon his lips, – that he *made* out of him something which even a Mithras priest could understand.... This was his moment of Damascus: he saw that he had *need* of the belief in immortality in order to depreciate 'the world', that the notion of 'hell' would become master of Rome, that with a 'Beyond' *this life* can be killed.... Nihilist and Christian, – they rhyme in German, and they do not only rhyme.

59

The whole labour of the ancient world *in vain*: I am at a loss for a word which could express my feelings at something so atrocious. – And in view of the fact that its labour was only preparatory, that with adamantine self-consciousness it laid the substructure, alone, to a work which was to last millenniums, the whole *significance* of the ancient world was certainly in vain!... What was the use of the Greeks? what was the use of the Romans? – All the prerequisites of a learned culture, all the scientific methods already existed, the great and peerless art of reading well had already been established – that indispensable condition to tradition, to culture and to scientific unity; natural science hand in hand with mathematics and mechanics was on the best possible road, – the sense for facts, the last and most valuable of all senses, had its schools, and its tradition was already centuries old! Is this understood? Everything *essential* had been discovered to make it possible for work to be begun: – methods, and this cannot be said too often, are the essential thing, also the most difficult thing, while they moreover have to wage the longest war against custom and indolence. That which today we have successfully reconquered for ourselves, by dint of unspeakable self-discipline – for in some way or other all of us still have the bad instincts, the Christian instincts, in our body, – the impartial eye for reality, the cautious hand, patience and seriousness in the smallest details, complete *uprightness* in knowledge, – all this was already there; it had been there over two thousand years before! And in addition to this there was also that excellent and subtle tact and taste! *Not* in the form of brain drilling! *Not* in the form of 'German' culture with the manners of a boor! But incarnate, manifesting itself in men's bearing and in their instinct, – in short constituting reality.... *All this in vain*! In one night it became merely a memory! – The Greeks! The Romans! Instinctive nobility, instinctive taste, methodic research, the genius of organisation and administration, faith, the *will* to the future of mankind, the great yea to all things materialised in the *imperium Romanum*, become visible to all the senses, grand style no longer manifested in mere art, but in reality, in truth, in *life*. – And buried in a night, not by a natural catastrophe! Not stamped to death by Teutons and other heavy-footed vandals! But destroyed by crafty, stealthy, invisible anæmic vampires! Not conquered, – but only drained of blood!... The concealed lust of revenge, miserable envy become *master*! Everything wretched, inwardly ailing, and full of ignoble feelings, the whole Ghetto-world of souls, was in a trice *uppermost*! – One only needs to read any one of the Christian agitators – St Augustine, for instance, – in order to realise, in order to smell, what filthy fellows came to the top in this movement. You would deceive yourselves utterly if you supposed that the leaders of the Christian agitation showed any lack of understanding – Ah! they were shrewd,

THE TWILIGHT OF THE IDOLS AND THE ANTICHRIST

shrewd to the point of holiness were these dear old Fathers of the Church! What they lack is something quite different. Nature neglected them, – it forgot to give them a modest dowry of decent, of respectable and of *cleanly* instincts.... Between ourselves, they are not even men. If Islam despises Christianity, it is justified a thousand times over; for Islam presupposes men.

60

Christianity destroyed the harvest we might have reaped from the culture of antiquity, later it also destroyed our harvest of the culture of Islam. The wonderful Moorish world of Spanish culture, which in its essence is more closely related to *us*, and which appeals more to our sense and taste than Rome and Greece, was *trampled to death* (– I do not say by what kind of feet), why? – because it owed its origin to noble, to manly instincts, because it said yea to life, even that life so full of the rare and refined luxuries of the Moors!... Later on the Crusaders waged war upon something before which it would have been more seemly in them to grovel in the dust, – a culture, beside which even our nineteenth century would seem very poor and very 'senile'. – Of course they wanted booty: the Orient was rich.... For goodness' sake let us forget our prejudices! Crusades – superior piracy, that is all! German nobility – that is to say, a Viking nobility at bottom, was in its element in such wars: the Church was only too well aware of how German nobility is to be won.... German nobility was always the 'Swiss Guard' of the Church, always at the service of all the bad instincts of the Church; but it was *well paid for it all*.... Fancy the Church having waged its deadly war upon everything noble on earth, precisely with the help of German swords, German blood and courage! A host of painful *questions* might be raised on this point German nobility scarcely takes a place in the history of higher culture: the reason of this is obvious; Christianity, alcohol – the two *great* means of corruption. As a matter of fact choice ought to be just as much out of the question between Islam and Christianity, as between an Arab and a Jew. The decision is already self-evident; nobody is at liberty to exercise a choice in this matter. A man is either of the Chandala or he is *not*... 'War with Rome to the knife! Peace and friendship with Islam': this is what that great free spirit, that genius among German emperors, – Frederick the Second, not only felt but also *did*.

What? Must a German in the first place be a genius, a free-spirit, in order to have *decent* feelings? I cannot understand how a German was ever able to have *Christian* feelings.

61

Here it is necessary to revive a memory which will be a hundred times more painful to Germans. The Germans have destroyed the last great harvest of culture which was to be garnered for Europe, – it destroyed the *Renaissance*. Does anybody at last understand, will anybody understand what the Renaissance was? *The transvaluation of Christian values*, the attempt undertaken with all means, all instincts and all genius to make the *opposite* values, the *noble* values triumph…. Hitherto there has been only *this* great war: there has never yet been a more decisive question than the Renaissance, – *my* question is the question of the Renaissance: – there has never been a more fundamental, a more direct and a more severe *attack*, delivered with a whole front upon the centre of the foe. To attack at the decisive quarter, at the very seat of Christianity, and there to place *noble* values on the throne, – that is to say, to *introduce* them into the instincts, into the most fundamental needs and desires of those sitting there…. I see before me a possibility perfectly magic in its charm and glorious colouring – it seems to me to scintillate with all the quivering grandeur of refined beauty, that there is an art at work within it which is so divine, so infernally divine, that one might seek through millenniums in vain for another such possibility; I see a spectacle so rich in meaning and so wonderfully paradoxical to boot, that it would be enough to make all the gods of Olympus rock with immortal laughter, – *Cæsar Borgia as Pope*…. Do you understand me?… Very well then, this would have been the triumph which I alone am longing for today: – this would have swept Christianity *away*! – What happened? A German monk, Luther, came to Rome. This monk, with all the vindictive instincts of an abortive priest in his body, foamed with rage over the Renaissance in Rome…. Instead of, with the profoundest gratitude, understanding the vast miracle that had taken place, the overcoming of Christianity at its *headquarters*, – the fire of his hate knew only how to draw fresh fuel from this spectacle. A religious man thinks only of himself. – Luther saw the corruption of the Papacy when the very reverse stared him in the face: the old corruption, the *peccatum originale*, Christianity *no longer* sat upon the Papal chair! But life! The triumph of life! The great yea to all lofty, beautiful and daring things!... And Luther reinstated the Church; he attacked it. The Renaissance thus became an event without meaning, a great *in vain*! – Ah these Germans, what have they not cost us already! In vain – this has always been the achievement of the Germans. – The Reformation, Leibniz, Kant and so-called German philosophy, the Wars of Liberation, the Empire – in each case are in vain for something which had already existed, for something which *cannot be recovered*.... I confess it, these Germans are my enemies: I despise every sort of uncleanliness in concepts and valuations in them, every kind of cowardice in the face of every honest yea or nay. For almost one thousand years, now, they have tangled and confused everything they have laid their hands on; they have on their conscience all the half-measures, all the three-eighth measures of which Europe is sick; they also have the most unclean, the most incurable, and the most irrefutable kind of Christianity – Protestantism – on their conscience.... If we shall never be able to get rid of Christianity, the *Germans* will be to blame.

62

With this I will now conclude and pronounce my judgment. I *condemn* Christianity and confront it with the most terrible accusation that an accuser has ever had in his mouth. To my mind it is the greatest of all conceivable corruptions, it has had the will to the last imaginable corruption. The Christian Church allowed nothing to escape from its corruption; it converted every value into its opposite, every truth into a lie, and every honest impulse into an ignominy of the soul. Let anyone dare to speak to me of its humanitarian blessings! To *abolish* any sort of distress was opposed to its profoundest interests; its very existence depended on states of distress; it created states of distress in order to make itself immortal.... The cancer germ of sin, for instance: the Church was the first to enrich mankind with this misery! – The 'equality of souls before God', this falsehood, this *pretext* for the *rancunes* of all the base-minded, this anarchist bomb of a concept, which has ultimately become the revolution, the modern idea, the principle of decay of the whole of social order, – this is *Christian* dynamite... The 'humanitarian' blessings of Christianity! To breed a self-contradiction, an art of self-profanation, a will to lie at any price, an aversion, a contempt of all good and honest instincts out of *humanitas*! Is this what you call the blessings of Christianity? – Parasitism as the only method of the Church; sucking all the blood, all the love, all the hope of life out of mankind with anæmic and sacred ideals. A 'Beyond' as the will to deny all reality; the cross as the trademark of the most subterranean form of conspiracy that has ever existed, – against health, beauty, well-constitutedness, bravery, intellect, kindliness of soul, *against life itself....*

This eternal accusation against Christianity I would fain write on all walls, wherever there are walls, – I have letters with which I can make even the blind see.... I call Christianity the one great curse, the one enormous and innermost perversion, the one great instinct of revenge, for which no means are too venomous, too underhand, too underground and too *petty*, – I call it the one immortal blemish of mankind....

And *time* is reckoned from the *dies nefastus* upon which this fatality came into being – from the first day of Christianity! – *why not rather from its last day? – From today?* – Transvaluation of all values!...

THE ETERNAL RECURRENCE AND EXPLANATORY NOTES TO *THUS SPAKE ZARATHUSTRA*.

TRANSLATOR'S PREFACE

The notes concerning the Eternal Recurrence, in this volume, are said by Mrs Foerster-Nietzsche to have been the first that Nietzsche ever wrote on the subject of his great doctrine. This being so, they must have been composed towards the autumn of the year 1881.

I have already pointed out elsewhere (*Will to Power*, vol. ii., Translator's Preface) how much importance Nietzsche himself ascribed to this doctrine, and how, until the end, he regarded it as the inspiration which had led to his chief work, *Thus Spake Zarathustra*. For the details relating to its inception, however, I would refer the reader to Mrs Foerster-Nietzsche's Introduction to her brother's chief work, which was translated for the eleventh volume of this Edition of the Complete Works.

In reading these notes it would be well to refer to Nietzsche's other utterances on the subject which are to be found at the end of vol. ii. of the *Will to Power*, and also, if possible, to have recourse to the original German text. Despite the greatest care, I confess that in some instances, I have felt a little doubt as to the precise English equivalent for the thoughts expressed under the heading *Eternal Recurrence*; and, though I have attributed this difficulty to the extreme novelty of the manner in which the subject is presented, it is well that the reader should be aware that such doubt has been entertained. For I disbelieve utterly in mere verbal translation, however accurate, and would question anybody's right to convert a German sentence into English – even though he were so perfect in both languages as to be almost absolutely bilingual, – if he did not completely grasp the thought behind the sentence.

The writing of the collected Explanatory Notes to *Thus Spake Zarathustra*, cannot be given any exact date. Some of them consist of comments, written down by Nietzsche after the completion of the book, and kept as the nucleus of an actual commentary to Zarathustra, which it seems to have been his intention, one day, to write; while others are merely memoranda and rough sketches, probably written before the completion of the work, and which served the purpose of a draft of his original plan. The reader who knows *Thus Spake Zarathustra* will be able to tell wherein the book ultimately differed from the plan visible in these preliminary notes.

As an authoritative, though alas! all too fragmentary elucidation of a few of the more obscure passages of Zarathustra, some of these notes are of the greatest value; and, in paragraph 73, for instance, there is an interpretation of the Fourth and Last Part, which I myself would have welcomed with great enthusiasm, at the time when I was having my first struggles with the spirit of this great German sage's life work.

ANTHONY M. LUDOVICI.

THE ETERNAL RECURRENCE

1. THE DOCTRINE EXPOUNDED AND SUBSTANTIATED

1

The extent of universal energy is limited; it is not 'infinite': we should beware of such excesses in our concepts! Consequently the number of states, changes, combinations, and evolutions of this energy, although it may be enormous and practically incalculable, is at any rate definite and not unlimited. The time, however, in which this universal energy works its changes is infinite – that is to say, energy remains eternally the same and is eternally active: – at this moment an infinity has already elapsed, that is to say, every possible evolution must already have taken place. Consequently the present process of evolution must be a repetition, as was also the one before it, as will also be the one which will follow. And so on forwards and backwards! Inasmuch as the entire state of all forces continually returns, everything has existed an infinite number of times. Whether, apart from this, anything exactly like something that formerly existed has ever appeared, is completely beyond proof. It would seem that each complete state of energy forms all qualities afresh even to the smallest degree, so that two different complete states could have nothing in common. Is it to be supposed that in one and the same complete states two precisely similar things could appear – for instance two leaves? I doubt it: it would take for granted that they had both had an absolutely similar origin, and in that case we should have to assume that right back in infinity two similar things had also existed despite all the changes in the complete states and their creation of new qualities – an impossible assumption.

2

Formerly it was thought that unlimited energy was a necessary corollary to unlimited activity in time, and that this energy could be exhausted by no form of consumption. Now it is thought that energy remains constant and does not require to be infinite. It is eternally active but it is no longer able eternally to create new forms, it must repeat itself: that is my conclusion.

3

An incalculable number of complete states of energy have existed, but these have not been infinitely different: for if they had been, unlimited energy would have been necessary. The energy of the universe can only have a given number of possible qualities.

4

The endless evolution of new forms is a contradiction, for it would imply eternally increasing energy. But whence would it grow? Whence would it derive its nourishment and its surplus of nourishment? The assumption that the universe is an organism contradicts the very essence of the organic.

5

In what principle and belief is that decisive turning point in philosophical thought best expressed which has come into being thanks to the preponderance of the scientific spirit over the religious and God-creating one? We insist upon the fact that the world as a sum of energy must not be regarded as unlimited – we forbid ourselves the concept infinite energy, because it seems incompatible with the concept energy.

6

An unlimited number of new changes and states on the part of limited energy is a contradiction, however extensive one may imagine it to be, and however economical the changes may be, provided it is infinite. We are therefore forced to conclude: (1) either that the universe began its activity at a given moment of time and will end in a similar fashion, – but the beginning of activity is absurd; if a state of equilibrium had been reached it would have persisted to all eternity; (2) Or there is no such thing as an endless number of changes, but a circle consisting of a definite number of them which continually recurs: activity is eternal, the number of the products and states of energy is limited.

7

If all the possible combinations and relations of forces had not already been exhausted, then an infinity would not yet lie behind us. Now since infinite time must be assumed, no fresh possibility can exist and everything must have appeared already, and moreover an infinite number of times.

8

The present world of forces leads back to a state of greatest simplicity in these forces: it likewise leads forwards to such a state, – cannot and must not *both* states be identical? No incalculable number of states can evolve out of a system of limited forces, that is to say, out of a given quantity of energy which may be precisely measured. Only when we falsely assume that space is unlimited, and that therefore energy gradually becomes dissipated, can the final state be an unproductive and lifeless one.

9

First principles. – The last physical state of energy which we can imagine must necessarily be the first also. The absorption of energy in latent energy must be the cause of the production of the most vital energy. For a highly positive state must follow a negative state. Space like matter is a subjective form, time is not. The notion of space first arose from the assumption that space could be empty. But there is no such thing as empty space. Everything is energy.

We cannot think of that which moves and that which is moved together, but both these things constitute matter and space. We isolate.

10

Concerning the resurrection of the world. – Out of two negatives, when they are forces, a positive arises. (Darkness comes of light opposed to light, cold arises from warmth opposed to warmth, &c., &c.)

11

An uncertain state of equilibrium occurs just as seldom in nature as two absolutely equal triangles. Consequently anything like a static state of energy in general is impossible. If stability were possible it would already have been reached.

12

Either complete equilibrium must in itself be an impossibility, or the changes of energy introduce themselves in the circular process before that equilibrium which is in itself possible has appeared. – But it would be madness to ascribe a feeling of self-preservation to existence! And the same applies to the conception of a contest of pain and pleasure among atoms.

13

Physics supposes that energy may be divided up: but every one of its possibilities must first be adjusted to reality. There can therefore be no question of dividing energy into equal parts; in every one of its states it manifests a certain quality, and qualities cannot be subdivided: hence a state of equilibrium in energy is impossible.

14

If energy had ever reached a stage of equilibrium that stage would have persisted: it has therefore never reached such a stage. The present condition of things contradicts this assumption. If we assume that there has ever been a state absolutely like the present one this assumption is in no wise refuted by the present state. For, among all the endless possibilities, this case must already have occurred, as an infinity is already behind us. If equilibrium were possible it would already have been reached. – And if this momentary state has already existed then that which bore it and the previous one also would likewise have existed and so on backwards, – and from this it follows that it has already existed not only twice but three times, – just as it will exist again not only twice but three times, – in fact an infinite number of times backwards and forwards. That is to say, the whole process of Becoming consists of a repetition of a definite number of precisely similar states. – Clearly the human brain cannot be left to imagine the whole series of possibilities: but in any case, quite apart from our ability to judge or our inability to conceive the whole range of possibilities, the present state at least is a possible one – because it is a real one. We should therefore say: in the event of the number of possibilities not being infinite, and assuming that in the course of unlimited time a limited number of these must appear, all real states must have been preceded by similar states? Because from every given moment a whole infinity is to be calculated backwards? The stability of forces and their equilibrium is a possible alternative: but it has not been reached; consequently the number of possibilities is greater than the number of real states. The fact that nothing similar recurs could not be explained by appealing to accident, but only by supposing that a certain intention, that no similar things should recur, were actually inherent in the essence of energy: for, if we grant that the number of cases is enormous, the occurrence of like cases is more probable than absolute disparity.

15

Let us think backwards a moment. If the world had a goal, this goal must have been reached: if a certain (unintentional) final state existed for the world, this state also would have been reached. If it were in any way capable of a stationary or stable condition, and if in the whole course of its existence only one second of Being, in the strict sense of the word, had been possible, then there could no longer be such a process as evolution, and therefore no thinking and no observing of such a process. If on the other hand the world were something which continually renovated itself, it would then be understood to be something miraculous and free to create itself – in fact something divine. Eternal renovation presupposes that energy voluntarily increases itself, that it not only has the intention, but also the power, to avoid repeating itself or to avoid returning into a previous form, and that every instant it adjusts itself in every one of its movements to prevent such a contingency, – or that it was incapable of returning to a state it had already passed through. That would mean that the whole sum of energy was not constant, any more than its attributes were. But a sum of energy which would be inconstant and which would fluctuate is quite unthinkable. Let us not indulge our fancy any longer with unthinkable things in order to fall once more before the concept of a Creator (multiplication out of nothing, reduction out of nothing, absolute arbitrariness and freedom in growth and in qualities): –

16

He who does not believe in the circular process of the universe must pin his faith to an arbitrary God – thus my doctrine becomes necessary as opposed to all that has been said hitherto in matters of Theism.

17

The hypothesis which I would oppose to that of the eternal circular process: – Would it be just as possible to explain the laws of the mechanical world as exceptions and seemingly as accidents among the things of the universe, as one possibility only among an incalculable number of possibilities? Would it be possible to regard ourselves as accidentally thrust into this corner of the mechanical universal arrangement? – That all chemical philosophy is likewise an exception and an accident in the world's economy, and finally that organic life is a mere exception and accident in the chemical world? Should we have to assume as the most general form of existence a world which was not yet mechanical, which was outside all mechanical laws (although accessible to them)? – and that as a matter of fact this world would be the most general now and for evermore, so that the origin of the mechanical world would be a lawless game which would ultimately acquire such consistency as the organic laws seem to have now from our point of view? So that all our mechanical laws would be not eternal, but evolved, and would have survived innumerable different mechanical laws, or that they had attained supremacy in isolated corners of the world and not in others? – It would seem that we need caprice, actual lawlessness, and only a capacity for law, a primeval state of stupidity which is not even able to concern itself with mechanics? The origin of qualities presupposes the existence of quantities, and these, for their part, might arise from a thousand kinds of mechanical processes.

Is not the existence of some sort of irregularity and incomplete circular form in the world about us, a sufficient refutation of the regular circularity of everything that exists? Whence comes this variety within the circular process? Is not everything far too complicated to have been the outcome of unity? And are not the many chemical laws and likewise the organic species and forms inexplicable as the result of homogeneity? or of duality? – Supposing there were such a thing as a regular contracting energy in all the centres of force in the universe, the question would be, whence could the most insignificant difference spring? For then the whole world would have to be resolved into innumerable completely equal rings and spheres of existence and we should have an incalculable number of exactly equal worlds side by side. Is it necessary for me to assume this? Must I suppose that an eternal sequence of like worlds also involves eternal juxtaposition of like worlds? But the multifariousness and disorder in the world which we have known hitherto contradicts this; no such universal similarity has existed in evolution, for in that case even for our part of the cosmos a regular spherical form must have been formed. Should the production of qualities not be subject to any strict laws? Can it be possible that different things have been derived from 'energy'? Arbitrarily? Is the conformity to law which we observe perhaps only a deception? Is it possible that it is not a primeval law? Is it possible that the multifariousness of qualities even in our part of the world is the result of the absolute occurrence of arbitrary characteristics? But that these characteristics no longer appear in our corner of the globe? Or that our corner of existence has adopted a rule which we call cause and effect when all the while it is no such thing (an arbitrary phenomenon become a rule, as for instance oxygen and hydrogen in chemistry)??? Is this rule simply a protracted kind of mood?

18

If the universe had been able to become an organism it would have become one already. As a whole we must try and regard it in the light of a thing as remote as possible from the organic. I believe that even our chemical affinity and coherence may be perhaps recently evolved and that these appearances only occur in certain corners of the universe at certain epochs. Let us believe in absolute necessity in the universe but let us guard against postulating any sort of law, even if it be a primitive and mechanical one of our own experience, as ruling over the whole and constituting one of its eternal characteristics. – All chemical qualities might have been evolved and might disappear and return. Innumerable characteristics might have been developed which for us, – from our limited point of view in time and space, defy observation. The transformation of a chemical quality may perhaps now be taking place, but so slowly that it escapes our most delicate calculations.

19

Inorganic matter, even though in most cases it may once have been organic, can have stored up no experience, – it is always without a past! If the reverse were the case a repetition would be impossible – for then matter would for ever be producing new qualities with new pasts.

20

We must guard against ascribing any aspiration or any goal to this circular process: Likewise we must not, from the point of view of our own needs, regard it as either monotonous or foolish, &c. We may grant that the greatest possible irrationality, as also its reverse, may be an essential feature of it: but we must not value it according to this hypothesis. Rationality or irrationality cannot stand as attributes of the universe. – We must not think of the law of this circular process as a thing evolved, by drawing false analogies with the circular motions occurring *within* the circle. There was no primitive chaos followed gradually by a more harmonious and finally definite circular motion of all forces: On the contrary everything is eternal and unevolved. If there ever was a chaos of forces, then that chaos itself was eternal and was repeated at its particular moment of time in the turn of the world wheel. The circular process is not the outcome of evolution, it is a primitive principle like the quantum of energy, and allows of no exception or violation. All Becoming takes place within the circular process and the quantum of energy which constitutes it: therefore we must not apply ephemeral processes like those for instance of heavenly bodies, of the ebb and flow of tides, of day and night, of the seasons, to the drawing of analogies for characterising the eternal circular process.

21

The 'chaos of the universe', inasmuch as it excludes any aspiration to a goal, does not oppose the thought of the circular process: the latter is simply an irrational necessity, absolutely free from any formal ethical or æsthetical significance. Arbitrariness in small things as in great is completely lacking here.

22

Let us guard against believing that the universe has a tendency to attain to certain forms, or that it aims at becoming more beautiful, more perfect, more complicated! All that is anthropomorphism! Anarchy, ugliness, form – are unrelated concepts. There is no such thing as imperfection in the realm of mechanics.

Everything has returned: Sirius, and the spider, and thy thoughts at this moment, and this last thought of thine that all these things will return.

23

Our whole world consists of the ashes of an incalculable number of living creatures: and even if living matter is ever so little compared with the whole, everything has already been transformed into life once before and thus the process goes on. If we grant eternal time we must assume the eternal change of matter.

24

Whoever thou mayest be, beloved stranger, whom I meet here for the first time, avail thyself of this happy hour and of the stillness around us, and above us, and let me tell thee something of the thought which has suddenly risen before me like a star which would fain shed down its rays upon thee and every one, as befits the nature of light. –

25

The world of energy suffers no diminution: otherwise with eternal time it would have grown weak and finally have perished altogether. The world of energy suffers no stationary state, otherwise this would already have been reached, and the clock of the universe would be at a standstill. The world of energy does not therefore reach a state of equilibrium; for no instant in its career has it had rest; its energy and its movement have been the same for all time. Whatever state this world could have reached must ere now have been attained, and not only once but an incalculable number of times. This applies to this very moment. It has already been here once before, and several times, and will recur in the same way, with all forces distributed as they are today: and the same holds good of the moment of time which bore the present and of that which shall be the child of the present. Fellow-man! Your whole life, like a sandglass, will always be reversed and will ever run out again, – a long minute of time will elapse until all those conditions out of which you were evolved return in the wheel of the cosmic process. And then you will find every pain and every pleasure, every friend and every enemy, every hope and every error, every blade of grass and every ray of sunshine once more, and the whole fabric of things that makes up your life. This ring in which you are but a grain will glitter afresh for ever. And in every one of these cycles of human life there will be one hour where for the first time one man, and then many, will perceive the mighty thought of the eternal recurrence of all things: – and for mankind this is always the hour of Noon.

2. THE EFFECTS OF THE DOCTRINE UPON MANKIND

26

How can we give weight to our inner life without making it evil and fanatical towards people who think otherwise. Religious belief is declining and man is beginning to regard himself as ephemeral and unessential, a point of view which is making him weak; he does not exercise so much effort in striving or enduring. What he wants is momentary enjoyment. He would make things light for himself, – and a good deal of his spirit gets squandered in this endeavour.

27

The political mania at which I smile just as merrily as my contemporaries smile at the religious mania of former times is above all Materialism, a belief in the world, and in the repudiation of a 'Beyond', of a 'back-world'. The object of those who believe in the latter is the well-being of the ephemeral individual: that is why Socialism is its fruit; for with Socialism ephemeral individuals wish to secure their happiness by means of socialisation. They have no reason to wait, as those men had who believed in eternal souls, in eternal development and eternal amelioration. My doctrine is: Live so that thou mayest desire to live again, – that is thy duty, – for in any case thou wilt live again. He unto whom striving is the greatest happiness, let him strive; he unto whom peace is the greatest happiness, let him rest; he unto whom subordination, following, obedience, is the greatest happiness, let him obey. All that is necessary is that he should know what it is that gives him the highest happiness, and to fight shy of no means! Eternity is at stake!

28

'But if everything is necessary, what control have I over my actions?' Thought and faith are a form of ballast which burden thee in addition to other burdens thou mayest have, and which are even more weighty than the latter. Sayest thou that nutrition, the land of thy birth, air, and society change thee and determine thee? Well, thy opinions do this to a much greater degree, for they even prescribe thy nourishment, thy land of adoption, thy atmosphere, and thy society for thee. – If thou ever assimilatest the thought of thoughts it will also alter thee. The question which thou wilt have to answer before every deed that thou doest: 'is this such a deed as I am prepared to perform an incalculable number of times?' is the best ballast.

29

The mightiest of all thoughts absorbs a good deal of energy which formerly stood at the disposal of other aspirations, and in this way it exercises a modifying influence; it creates new laws of motion in energy, though no new energy. But it is precisely in this respect that there lies some possibility of determining new emotions and new desires in men.

30

Let us try and discover how the thought that something gets repeated has affected mankind hitherto (the year, for instance, or periodical illnesses, waking and sleeping, &c.). Even supposing the recurrence of the cycle is only a probability or a possibility, even a thought, even a possibility, can shatter us and transform us. It is not only feelings and definite expectations that do this! See what effect the thought of eternal damnation has had!

31

From the moment when this thought begins to prevail all colours will change their hue and a new history will begin.

32

The history of the future: this thought will tend to triumph ever more and more, and those who disbelieve in it will be forced, according to their nature, ultimately to die out.

He, alone, who will regard his existence as capable of eternal recurrence will remain over: but among such as these a state will be possible of which the imagination of no utopist has ever dreamt!

33

Ye fancy that ye will have a long rest ere your second birth takes place, – but do not deceive yourselves! 'Twixt your last moment of consciousness and the first ray of the dawn of your new life no time will elapse, – as a flash of lightning will the space go by, even though living creatures think it is billions of years, and are not even able to reckon it. Timelessness and immediate re-birth are compatible, once intellect is eliminated!

34

Thou feelest that thou must soon take thy leave perhaps – and the sunset glow of this feeling pierces through thy happiness. Give heed to this sign: it means that thou lovest life and thyself, and life as it has hitherto affected thee and moulded thee, – and that thou cravest for its eternity – *Non alia sed hæc vita sempiterna!*

Know also, that transiency singeth its short song for ever afresh and that at the sound of the first verse thou wilt almost die of longing when thou thinkest that it might be for the last time.

35

Let us stamp the impress of eternity upon our lives! This thought contains more than all the religions which taught us to contemn this life as a thing ephemeral, which bade us squint upwards to another and indefinite existence. –

36

We must not strive after distant and unknown states of bliss and blessings and acts of grace, but we must live so that we would fain live again and live for ever so, to all eternity! – Our duty is present with us every instant.

37

The leading tendencies: (1) We must implant the love of life, the love of every man's own life in every conceivable way! However each individual may understand this love of self his neighbour will acquiesce, and will have to learn great tolerance towards it: however much it may often run counter to his taste, – provided the individual in question really helps to increase his joy in his own life!

(2) We must all be one in our hostility towards everything and everybody who tends to cast a slur upon the value of life: towards all gloomy, dissatisfied and brooding natures. We must prevent these from procreating! But our hostility itself must be a means to our joy! Thus

we shall laugh; we shall mock and we shall exterminate without bitterness! Let this be our mortal combat.

This life is thy eternal life!

38

What was the cause of the downfall of the Alexandrian culture? With all its useful discoveries and its desire to investigate the nature of this world, it did not know how to lend this life its ultimate importance, the thought of a Beyond was more important to it! To teach anew in this regard is still the most important thing of all: – perhaps if metaphysics are applied to this life in the most emphatic way, – as in the case of my doctrine!

39

This doctrine is lenient towards those who do not believe in it. It speaks of no hells and it contains no threats. He who does not believe in it has but a fleeting life in his consciousness.

40

It would be terrible if we still believed in sin, but whatever we may do, however often we may repeat it, it is all innocent. If the thought of the eternal recurrence of all things does not overwhelm thee, then it is not thy fault: and if it does overwhelm thee, this does not stand to thy merit either. – We think more leniently of our forebears than they themselves thought of themselves; we mourn over the errors which were to them constitutional; but we do not mourn over their evil.

41

Let us guard against teaching such a doctrine as if it were a suddenly discovered religion! It must percolate through slowly, and whole generations must build on it and become fruitful through it, – in order that it may grow into a large tree which will shelter all posterity. What are the two thousand years in which Christianity has maintained its sway? For the mightiest thought of all many millenniums will be necessary, – long, long, long will it have to remain puny and weak!

42

For this thought we do not require thirty years of glory with drums and fifes, and thirty years of grave-digging followed by an eternity of macaberesque stillness, as is the case with so many other famous thoughts.

Simple and well-nigh arid as it is, this thought must not even require eloquence to uphold it.

43

Are ye now prepared? Ye must have experienced every form of scepticism and ye must have wallowed with voluptuousness in ice-cold baths, – otherwise ye have no right to this thought; I wish to protect myself against those who are over-ready to believe, likewise against those who gush over anything! I would defend my doctrine in advance. It must be the religion of the freest, most cheerful and most sublime souls, a delightful pastureland somewhere between golden ice and a pure heaven!

EXPLANATORY NOTES TO THUS SPAKE ZARATHUSTRA

1

All goals have been annihilated: valuations are turning against each other:

People call him good who hearkens to the dictates of his own heart, but they also call him good who merely does his duty;

People call the mild and conciliating man good, but they also call him good who is brave, inflexible and severe;

People call him good who does not do violence to himself, but they also call the heroes of self-mastery good;

People call the absolute friend of truth good, but they also call him good who is pious and a transfigurer of things;

People call him good who can obey his own voice, but they also call the devout man good;

People call the noble and the haughty man good, but also him who does not despise and who does not assume condescending airs.

People call him good who is kindhearted and who steps out of the way of broils, but he who thirsts for fight and triumph is also called good;

People call him good who always wishes to be first, but they also call him good who does not wish to be ahead of anybody in anything.

2

We possess a powerful store of moral *feelings*, but we have no goal for them all. They mutually contradict each other: they have their origin in different tables of values.

There is a wonderful amount of moral power, but there is no longer any goal towards which all this power can be directed.

3

All goals have been annihilated, mankind must give themselves a fresh goal. It is an error to suppose that they had one: they gave themselves all the goals they ever had. But the prerequisites of all previous goals have been annihilated.

Science traces the course of things but points to no goal: what it does give consists of the fundamental facts upon which the new goal must be based.

4

The profound sterility of the nineteenth century. I have not encountered a single man who really had a new ideal to bring forward. The character of German music kept me hoping longest, but in vain. A stronger type in which all our powers are synthetically correlated – this constitutes my faith.

Apparently everything is decadence. We should so direct this movement of decline that it may provide the strongest with a new form of existence.

5

The dissolution of morality, in its practical consequences, leads to the atomistic individual, and further to the subdivision of the individual into a quantity of parts – absolute liquefaction.

That is why a goal is now more than ever necessary; and love, but a new love.

6

I say: 'As long as your morality hung over me I breathed like one asphyxiated. That is why I throttled this snake. I wished to live, consequently it had to die.'

7

As long as people are still *forced* to act, that is to say as long as commands are given, synthesis (the suppression of the moral man) will not be realised. To be unable to be otherwise: instincts and commanding reason extending beyond any immediate object: the ability to enjoy one's own nature in action.

8

None of them wish to bear the burden of the commander; but they will perform the most strenuous task if only thou commandest them.

9

We must overcome the past in ourselves: we must combine the instincts afresh and direct the whole together to one goal: an extremely difficult undertaking! It is not only the evil instincts which have to be overcome – the so-called good instincts must be conquered also and consecrated anew!

10

No leaps must be made in virtue! But everyone must be given a different path! Not leading to the highest development of each! Yet everyone may be a bridge and an example for others.

11

To help, to pity, to submit and to renounce personal attacks with a good will, – these things may make even insignificant and superficial men tolerable to the eye: such men must not be contradicted in their belief that this good will is 'virtue in itself'.

12

Man makes a deed valuable: but how might a deed make man valuable?

13

Morality is the concern of those who cannot free themselves from it: for such people morality therefore belongs to the conditions of existence. It is impossible to refute conditions of existence: the only thing one can do is not to have them.

14

If it were true that life did not deserve to be welcomed, the moral man, precisely on account of his self-denial and obligingness, would then be guilty of misusing his fellow to his own personal advantage.

15

'Love thy neighbour' – this would mean first and foremost: 'Let thy neighbour go his own way' – and it is precisely this kind of virtue that is the most difficult!

16

The bad man as the parasite. We must not be merely feasters and gourmets of life: this is ignoble.

17

It is a noble sense which forbids our being only feasters and gourmets of life – this sense revolts against hedonism – : we want to perform something in return! – But the fundamental feeling of the masses is that one must live for nothing, – that is their vulgarity.

18

The converse valuations hold good for the lower among men: in their case therefore it is necessary to implant virtues. They must be elevated above their lives, by means of absolute commands and terrible taskmasters.

19

What is required: the new law must be made practicable – and out of its fulfilment, the overcoming of this law, and higher law, must evolve. Zarathustra defines the attitude towards law, inasmuch as he suppresses the law of laws which is morality.

Laws as the backbone. They must be worked at and created, by being fulfilled. The slavish attitude which has reigned hitherto towards law!

20

The self-overcoming of Zarathustra as the prototype of mankind's self-overcoming for the benefit of Superman. To this end the overcoming of morality is necessary.

21

The type of the lawgiver, his development and his suffering. What is the purpose of giving laws at all?

Zarathustra is the herald who calls forth many lawgivers.

22

Individual instruments.

1. The Commanders, the mighty – who do not love, unless it be that they love the images according to which they create. The rich in

vitality, the versatile, the free, who overcome that which is extant.

2. The obedient, the 'emancipated' – love and reverence constitute their happiness, they have a sense of what is higher (their deficiencies are made whole by the sight of the lofty).

3. The slaves, the order of 'henchmen' – : they must be made comfortable, they must cultivate pity for one another.

23
The giver, the creator, the teacher – these are preludes of the ruler.

24
All virtue and all self-mastery has only one purpose: that of preparing for the ruler!

25
Every sacrifice that the ruler makes is rewarded a hundredfold.

26
How much does not the warrior, the prince, the man who is responsible for himself, sacrifice! – this should be highly honoured.

27
The terrible task of the ruler who educates himself: – the kind of man and people over which he will rule must be forecast in him: it is in himself therefore that he must first have become a ruler!

28
The great educator like nature must elevate obstacles in order that these may be overcome.

29
The new teachers as preparatory stages for the highest Architect (they must impose their type on things).

30
Institutions may be regarded as the after effects of great individuals and the means of giving great individuals root and soil – until the fruit ultimately appears.

31

As a matter of fact mankind is continually trying to be able to dispense with great individuals by means of corporations, &c. But they are utterly dependent upon such great individuals for their ideal.

32

The eudæmonistic and social ideals lead men backwards, – it may be that they aim at a very useful working class, – they are creating the ideal slave of the future, the lower caste which must on no account be lacking!

33

Equal rights for all! – this is the most extraordinary form of injustice, for with it the highest men do not get their due.

34

It is not a matter of the rights of the stronger, for strong and weak are alike in this, that they all extend their power as far as they can.

35

A new form of estimating man: above all the question:
How much power has he got?
How manifold are his instincts?
How great is his capacity for communication and assimilation?
The ruler as the highest type.

36

Zarathustra rejoices that the war of the classes is at last over, and that now at length the time is ripe for an order of rank among individuals. His hatred of the democratic system of levelling is only a blind; as a matter of fact he is very pleased that this has gone so far. Now he can perform his task. –

Hitherto his doctrines had been directed only at the ruling caste of the future. These lords of the earth must now take the place of God, and must create for themselves the profound and absolute confidence of those they rule. Their new holiness, their renunciation of happiness and ease, must be their first principle. To the lowest they grant the heirloom of happiness, not to themselves. They deliver the physiologically botched by teaching them the doctrine of 'swift death'. They offer religions and philosophical systems to each according to his rank.

37

'The conflict in the heart of the ruler is the contest between the love which is in his heart for him who is most remote, and the love which he feels for his neighbour.'

To be a creator and to be capable of goodness are not at all things which exclude one another. They are rather one and the same thing; but the creator is farsighted and the good man nearsighted.

38

The feeling of power. The strife of all egos to discover that thought which will remain poised above men like a star. – The ego is a *primum mobile*.

39

The struggle for the application of the power which mankind now represents! Zarathustra calls to the gladiators of this struggle.

40

We must make our ideals prevail: – We must strive for power in such a way as our ideal commands.

41

The doctrine of the Eternal Recurrence is the turning point of history.

42

Suddenly the terrible chamber of truth is opened, an unconscious self-protectiveness, caution, ambush, defence keeps us from the gravest knowledge. Thus have I lived heretofore. I suppress something; but the restless babbling and rolling down of stones has rendered my instinct over-powerful. Now I am rolling my last stone, the most appalling truth stands close to my hand. Truth has been exorcised out of its grave: – we created it, we waked it: the highest expression of courage and of the feeling of power. Scorn of all pessimism that has existed hitherto!

We fight with it, – we find out that our only means of enduring it is to create a creature who is able to endure it: – unless, of course, we voluntarily dazzle ourselves afresh and blind ourselves in regard to it. But this we are no longer able to do!

We it was who created the gravest thought, – let us now create a being unto whom it will be not only light but blessed.

In order to be able to create we must allow ourselves greater freedom than has ever been vouchsafed us before; to this end we must be emancipated from morality, and we must be relieved by means of feasts (Premonitions of the future! We must celebrate the future and no longer the past! We must compose the myth poetry of the future! We must live in hopes!) Blessed moments! And then we must once again pull down the curtain and turn our thoughts to the next unswerving purpose.

43

Mankind must set its goal above itself – not in a false world, however, but in one which would be a continuation of humanity.

44

The half-way house is always present when the will to the future arises: the greatest event stands immediately before it.

45

Our very essence is to create a being higher than ourselves. We must create beyond ourselves. That is the instinct of procreation, that is the instinct of action and of work. – Just as all willing presupposes a purpose, so does mankind presuppose a creature which is not yet formed but which provides the aim of life. This is the freedom of all will. Love, reverence, yearning for perfection, longing, all these things are inherent in a purpose.

46

My desire: to bring forth creatures which stand sublimely above the whole species man: and to sacrifice 'one's neighbours' and oneself to this end.

The morality which has existed hitherto was limited within the confines of the species: all moralities that have existed hitherto have been useful in the first place in order to give unconditional stability to this species: once this has been achieved the aim can be elevated.

One movement is absolute; it is nothing more than the levelling down of mankind, great ant-organisations, &c.

The other movement, my movement, is conversely the accentuation of all contrasts and gulfs, and the elimination of equality, together with the creation of supremely powerful creatures.

The first movement brings forth the last man, my movement brings forth the Superman. It is by no means the goal to regard the latter as the master of the first: two races ought to exist side by side, – separated as far asunder as possible; the one, like the Epicurean gods, not concerning themselves in the least with the others.

47

The opposite of the Superman is the last man: I created him simultaneously with the former.

48

The more an individual is free and firm, the more exacting becomes his love: at last he yearns for Superman, because nothing else is able to appease his love.

49

Half-way round the course Superman arises.

50

Among men I was frightened: among men I desired a host of things and nothing satisfied me. It was then that I went into solitude and created Superman. And when I had created him I draped him in the great veil of Becoming and let the light of midday shine upon him.

51

'We wish to create a Being', we all wish to have a hand in it, to love it. We all want to be pregnant – and to honour and respect ourselves on that account.

We must have a goal in view of which we may all love each other! All other goals are only fit for the scrap heap.

52

The strongest in body and soul are the best – Zarathustra's fundamental proposition – ; from them is generated that higher morality of the creator. Man must be regenerated after his own image: this is what he wants, this is his honesty.

53

Genius to Zarathustra seems like the incarnation of his thought.

54

Loneliness for a certain time is necessary in order that a creature may become completely permeated with his own soul – cured and hard. A new form of community would be one in which we should assert ourselves martially. Otherwise the spirit becomes tame. No Epicurean 'gardens' and mere 'retirement from the masses'. War (but without powder) between different thoughts and the hosts who support them!

A new nobility, the result of breeding. Feasts celebrating the foundation of families.

The day divided up afresh; bodily exercise for all ages. *Ἀγών* as a principle.

The love of the sexes as a contest around the principle in becoming and coming. – Ruling will be taught and practised, its hardness as well as its mildness. As soon as one faculty is acquired in a masterly manner another one must be striven after.

We must let ourselves be taught by the evil, and allow them an opportunity of a contest. We must make use of the degenerate. – The right of punishment will consist in this, that the offender may be used as an experimental subject (in dietetics): this is the consecration of punishment, that one man be used for the highest needs of a future being.

We protect our new community because it is the bridge to our ideal of the future. And for it we work and let others work.

55

The measure and mean must be found in striving to attain to something beyond mankind: the highest and strongest kind of man must be discovered! The highest tendency must be represented continually in small things: – perfection, maturity, rosy-cheeked health, mild discharges of power. Just as an artist works, must we apply ourselves to our daily task and bring ourselves to perfection in everything we do. We must be honest in acknowledging our real motives to ourselves, as is becoming in the mighty man.

56

No impatience! Superman is our next stage and to this end, to this limit, moderation and manliness are necessary.

Mankind must surpass itself, as the Greeks did – and no fleshless fantasies must be indulged. The higher mind which is associated with a sickly and nervous character must be suppressed. The goal: the higher culture of the whole body and not only of the brain.

57

'Man is something that must be surpassed': – it is a matter of tempo: the Greeks were wonderful, there was no haste about them. – My predecessors: Heraclitus, Empedocles, Spinoza, Goethe.

58

1. Dissatisfaction with ourselves. An antidote to repentance. The transformation of temperament (*e.g.*, by means of inorganic substances). Good will to this dissatisfaction. We should wait for our thirst and let it become great in order to discover its source.

2. Death must be transformed into a means of victory and triumph.

3. The attitude towards disease. Freedom where death is concerned.

4. The love of the sexes is a means to an ideal (it is the striving of a being to perish through his opposite). The love for a suffering deity.

5. Procreation is the holiest of all things. Pregnancy, the creation of a woman and a man, who wish to enjoy their unity, and erect a monument to it by means of a child.

6. Pity as a danger. Circumstances must be created which enable everyone to be able to help himself, and which leave him to choose whether he would be helped.

7. Education must be directed at making men evil, at developing their inner devil.

8. Inner war as 'development'.

9. 'The maintenance of the species', and the thought of eternal recurrence.

59

Principal doctrine. We must strive to make every stage one of perfection, and rejoice therein, – we must make no leaps!

In the first place, the promulgation of laws. After the Superman the doctrine of eternal recurrence will strike us with horror: Now it is endurable.

60

Life itself created this thought which is the most oppressive for life. Life wishes to get beyond its greatest obstacle!

We must desire to perish in order to arise afresh, – from one day to the other. Wander through a hundred souls, – let that be thy life and thy fate! And then finally: desire to go through the whole process once more!

61

The highest thing of all would be for us to be able to endure our immortality.

62

The moment in which I begot recurrence is immortal, for the sake of that moment alone I will endure recurrence.

63

The teaching of eternal recurrence – it is at first oppressive to the more noble souls and apparently a means of weeding them out, – then the inferior and less sensitive natures would remain over! 'This doctrine must be suppressed and Zarathustra killed.'

64

The hesitation of the disciples. 'We are already able to bear with this doctrine, but we should destroy the many by means of it!'

Zarathustra laughs: 'Ye shall be the hammer: I laid this hammer in your hands.'

65

I do not speak to you as I speak to the people. The highest thing for them would be to despise and to annihilate themselves: the next highest thing would be for them to despise and annihilate each other.

66

'My will to do good compels me to remain silent. But my will to the Superman bids me speak and sacrifice even my friends.'

'I would fain form and transform you, how could I endure things otherwise!'

67

The history of higher man. The rearing of the better man is incalculably more painful. The ideal of the necessary sacrifice which it involves, as in the case of Zarathustra, should be demonstrated: A man should leave his home, his family and his native land. Live under the scorn of the prevailing morality. The anguish of experiments and errors. The solution of all the joys offered by the older ideals (they are now felt to be partly hostile and partly strange).

68

What is it which gives a meaning, a value, an importance to things? It is the creative heart which yearns and which created out of this yearning. It created joy and woe. It wanted to sate itself also with woe. Every kind of pain that man or beast has suffered, we must take upon ourselves and bless, and have a goal whereby such suffering would acquire some meaning.

69

Principal doctrine: the transfiguration of pain into a blessing, and of poison into food, lies in our power. The will to suffering.

70

Concerning heroic greatness as the only state of pioneers. (A yearning for utter ruin as a means of enduring one's existence.)

We must not desire one state only; we must rather desire to be periodical creatures – like existence.

Absolute indifference to other people's opinions (because we know their weights and measures), but their opinions of themselves should be the subject of pity.

71

Disciples must unite three qualities in themselves: they must be true, they must be able and willing to be communicative, they must have profound insight into each other.

72

All kinds of higher men and their oppression and blighting (as a case in point, Duhring, who was ruined by isolation) – on the whole, this is the fate of higher men today, they seem to be a species that is condemned to die out: this fact seems to come to Zarathustra's ears like a great cry for help. All kinds of insane degenerations of higher natures seem to approach him (nihilism for instance).

73

Higher Men who come to Zarathustra in Despair.
Temptations to return prematurely to the world – thanks to the provocation of one's sympathies.

1. The rolling stone, the homeless one, the wanderer: – he who has unlearned the love of his people because he has learned to love many peoples, – the good European.

2. The gloomy, ambitious son of the people, shy, lonely, and ready for anything, – who chooses rather to be alone than to be a destroyer, – he offers himself as an instrument.

3. The ugliest man, who is obliged to adorn himself (historical sense) and who is always in search of a new garment: he desires to make his appearance becoming, and finally retires into solitude in order not to be seen, he is ashamed of himself.

4. He who honours facts ('the brain of a leech'), the most subtle intellectual conscience, and because he has it in excess, a guilty conscience, – he wants to get rid of himself.

5. The poet, who at bottom thirsts, for savage freedom, – he chooses loneliness and the severity of knowledge.

6. The discoverer of new intoxicants, – the musician, the sorcerer, who finally drops on his knees before a loving heart and says: 'Not to me do I wish to lead you but yonder to him.'

Those who are sober to excess and who have a yearning for intoxication which they do not gratify. The Supersobersides.

7. Genius (as an attack of insanity), becoming frozen through lack of love: 'I am neither a genius nor a god.' Great tenderness: 'people must show him more love!'

8. The rich man who has given everything away and who asks everybody: 'Have you anything you do not want? give me some of it!' as a beggar.

9. The Kings who renounce dominion: 'we seek him who is more worthy to rule' – against 'equality': the great man is lacking, consequently reverence is lacking too.

10. The actor of happiness.

11. The pessimistic soothsayer who detects fatigue everywhere.

12. The fool of the big city.

13. The youth from the mount.

14. The woman (seeks the man).

15. The envious emaciated toiler and *arriviste*.

16. The good,

17. The pious,

18. The self-centred and saints,

and their mad fancy: 'For God', that means 'For me.'

74

'I gave you the most weighty thought: maybe mankind will perish through it, perhaps also mankind will be elevated through it inasmuch as by its means the elements which are hostile to life will be overcome and eliminated.' 'Ye must not chide Life, but yourselves!' – The destiny of higher man is to be a creator. The organisation of higher men, the education of the future ruler. 'YE must rejoice in your superior power when ye rule and when ye form anew.' 'Not only man but Superman will recur eternally!'

75

The typical suffering of the reformer and also his consolations. The seven solitudes.

He lives as though he were beyond all ages: his loftiness allows him to have intercourse with the anchorites and the misunderstood of every age.

Only his beauty is his defence. He lays his hands on the next thousand years.

His love increases as he sees the impossibility of avoiding the affliction of pain with it.

76

Zarathustra's mood is not one of mad impatience for Superman! It is peaceful, it can wait: but all action has derived some purpose from being the road and means thither, – and must be done well and perfectly.

The repose of the great stream! Consecration of the smallest thing. All unrest, and violent longing, all loathing should be presented in the third part and be overcome! The gentleness, and mildness, &c., in the first and second parts are both signs of a power which is not yet self-reliant!

With the recovery of Zarathustra, Cæsar stands there inexorable and kind: – the gulf separating creation, goodness, and wisdom is annihilated.

Clearness, peace, no exaggerated craving, happiness in the moment which is properly occupied and immortalised!

77

Zarathustra, Part III.: 'I myself am happy.' – When he had taken leave of mankind he returned unto himself. Like a cloud it vanishes from him. The manner in which Superman must live: like an Epicurean God.

Divine suffering is the substance of the third part of Zarathustra. The human state of the legislator is only brought forward as an example.

His intense love for his friends seems to him a disease, – once more he becomes peaceful.

When the invitations come he gently evades them.

78

In the fourth part it is necessary to say precisely why it is that the time of the great noon has come: It is really a description of the age given by means of visits, but interpreted by Zarathustra.

In the fourth part it is necessary to say precisely why 'a chosen people' has first to be created: – they are the lucky cases of nature as opposed to the unlucky (exemplified by the visitors): only to them – the lucky cases – is Zarathustra able to express himself concerning ultimate problems, them alone is he able to inspire with activity on behalf of this theory. They are strong, healthy, hard and above all noble enough for him to give them the hammer with which to remould the whole world.

79

The unity in power of the creator, the lover and the knight of knowledge.

80

Love alone shall judge – (the creative love which forgets itself in its work).

81

Zarathustra can only dispense happiness once the order of rank is established. Therefore this doctrine must be taught first.

The order of rank develops into a system of earthly dominion: the lords of the earth come last, a new ruling caste. Here and there there arises from them a perfectly Epicurean God, a Superman, a transfigurer of existence.

The Superhuman's notion of the world. Dionysus. Returning from these most strange of all pursuits Zarathustra comes back with love to the narrowest and smallest things, – he blesses all his experiences and dies with a blessing on his lips.

82

From people who merely pray we must become people who bless.